Joe's Two Cents

It's Great to Be ALIVE!

By Joe Paradis

PETER E. RANDALL PUBLISHER LLC
Portsmouth, New Hampshire 03802
2007

© Copyright 2007 by Joe Paradis
All Rights Reserved.

Author Web site: www.joes2cents.com

ISBN10: 1-931807-63-9
ISBN13: 978-1-931807-63-0

Library of Congress Control Number: 2007936874

Peter E. Randall Publisher LLC
P.O. Box 4726
Portsmouth, NH 03802

www.perpublisher.com

book design: Grace Peirce

Photo credits
Front cover photo by Joanne Paradis
Back cover photo by Caitlin Southmayd

To my wonderful parents,
Leo and Rosemarie Paradis, from whom I inherited
two primary traits—
a keen sense of humor
and a knack for practicality.

May those family genes continue to flow through future generations.
Just watch out, world.

Thanks, Mom and Dad.

Contents

i.	Acknowledgments	vii
ii.	Introduction	ix
1	A Day of Beauty	3
2	The Junk Drawer	5
3	Baseball Etiquette	7
4	The Girls of Home Depot	10
5	If I Were a Yankees Fan	15
6	Two Boys and a Game	19
7	Redefining the Golden Years	23
8	The Family Christmas Letter	25
9	Splitting the Bill	29
10	I M, I Said (with apologies to Neil Diamond)	33
11	Selective Hearing	37
12	Collecting Manly Things	41
13	Domestic Chores for the Man	45
14	The Remote	47
15	Talking With the Hands	51
16	The Beach Date	55
17	A Taste of College, Maine Style	59
18	Dump Guys	63
19	A New Year's That Might Have Been	67
20	The Pause … Honoring Three Young Men Why We Have Heroes Remembering Justin A Tribute to Herbert	71
21	First Freedom	83
22	The Green, Green Grass of Home	85
23	Washing Your Hands—The Saving Grace	89
24	Matching Wits With a Tree Frog	93

25	Barbeque Man	97
26	Guys Night Out	101
27	The Family Pool Party, Part I	105
28	When the Boys Come to Call	109
29	A Bountiful Harvest	113
30	The Great Bathroom Debates	117
31	Another Year of Stringing the Lights	121
32	Girl Talk	125
33	Turning Fifty	129
34	The Trial Run	131
35	Steppin' Out	135
36	The Greatest Band Ever	139
37	What to Write About?	143
38	Shamelessly Gloating	147

Acknowledgments

I am deeply grateful to so many people who, knowingly or unknowingly, have contributed to the content of this book. First and foremost, I thank my wife Joanne and my children, Robert and Danielle, who have quite often been the inspiration for my stories. My wife, in particular, is a saint. She has let me survive to write another day.

I am also grateful to Deb and Chris Paul for allowing me the opportunity to write my column in their newspaper, *The Londonderry Times*. Without that vehicle, I would not have been able to make as many people laugh, and encourage them to read just for fun. I thank all those readers as well. Your wonderful comments continually inspire me to write the next story.

I thank all those, living or dead, who have become the memories of my life. Many of those memories have become the bases of my stories. I have come to realize that we all share similar experiences and when I write about mine, it's just plain cool to hear that a reader has experienced the same thing.

I thank "those who have gone before me," my fellow writers who have encouraged me to pursue my dream of writing a book. In particular, I am indebted to Jack Falvey, local writing icon and Super Salesman. Our non-stop chats over drinks and hors d'oeuvres have always been inspiring. We've not had a full course dinner yet, because we're both too cheap, but I suspect we'll splurge one of these days. I also thank John Clayton of *The Union Leader*, who has always been generous with his time and thoughts—whether about writing his own column or fixing his snow blower or bailing water from his basement. John is probably unaware of his real effect on those of us who aspire to do what he does exceptionally well.

I am grateful to Peter and Deidre Randall and the staff at Peter E. Randall Publisher for agreeing to take on my book project. They have been a joy to work with. There is no substitute for professionalism.

And finally, a personal note: Thanks, Lord, for all You have given me—my wonderful family, above all. I suppose I am living proof that there is much more to life than the material world. That's why I can laugh so much—and hopefully You can too.

Introduction

On a beautiful summer morning in August of 2000, I was frantically helping to blow up a bounce house just before the annual Old Home Day celebration in my hometown of Londonderry, New Hampshire. I was a marketing manager at the time, for our local cable company, and the bounce house was our way of helping to celebrate that traditional event. Suddenly, I heard a voice behind me asking if anyone knew Joe Paradis. I always cringe when I hear my name . . . it's usually my kids asking for money. It turned out to be Deb Paul, a new resident in town, who had just started a monthly hometown newspaper called the *Londonderry Times*. She'd been pursuing me for months, because she wanted the cable company to advertise with her paper—and we eventually did, once the paper went weekly. That's what building community is all about.

Three years later, Deb asked me if I wanted to write a humor column for her newspaper. "Something like Andy Rooney would do," as she put it. I certainly didn't think I was in Mr. Rooney's league, but I agreed, because I'd always loved to write. And so *Joe's Two Cents* was born.

Joe's Two Cents is rooted in finding humor among the things we experience in our daily lives. Most times, I think I succeed. It's very gratifying when someone comes up to me in the supermarket and says "You read my mind! That's exactly what I was thinking!" Thankfully, I haven't had to coach anyone to say that yet, although I once offered to pay for a can of peas in one lady's hand, when she approached me in the produce aisle, with a nice compliment.

Some liken my low key humorous approach to that of Jerry Seinfeld, for which I'm very flattered. Truth be told, I never watched his television show until it was in re-runs. Even then, I've probably seen only about a dozen of them—due to time constraints, rather than anything else. But personally, I think Seinfeld is the ultimate comedian—right there with Robin Williams. Jerry makes the ordinary laughable, without resorting to language that crosses the line—not too much anyhow. Maybe someday I'll be fortunate enough to meet him. Hopefully, before I'm sitting in my wheelchair on the front porch of some nursing home, sucking a lunch of mashed peas through a straw and drooling.

Within this book, I hereby present to you a collection of some of my favorite stories from *Joe's Two Cents*. I've added some pictures and a little introduction to each story, just to keep you awake. I've tried to accumulate those stories that my readers have told me are also their favorites—that would seem to be a good test of their staying power. See what you think. I'm just honored to be able to publish this collection and hopefully follow it with several more.

Enjoy—because we all need to laugh at ourselves a bit more. Remember, it's great to be alive!

Joe's Two Cents

It's Great to Be ALIVE!

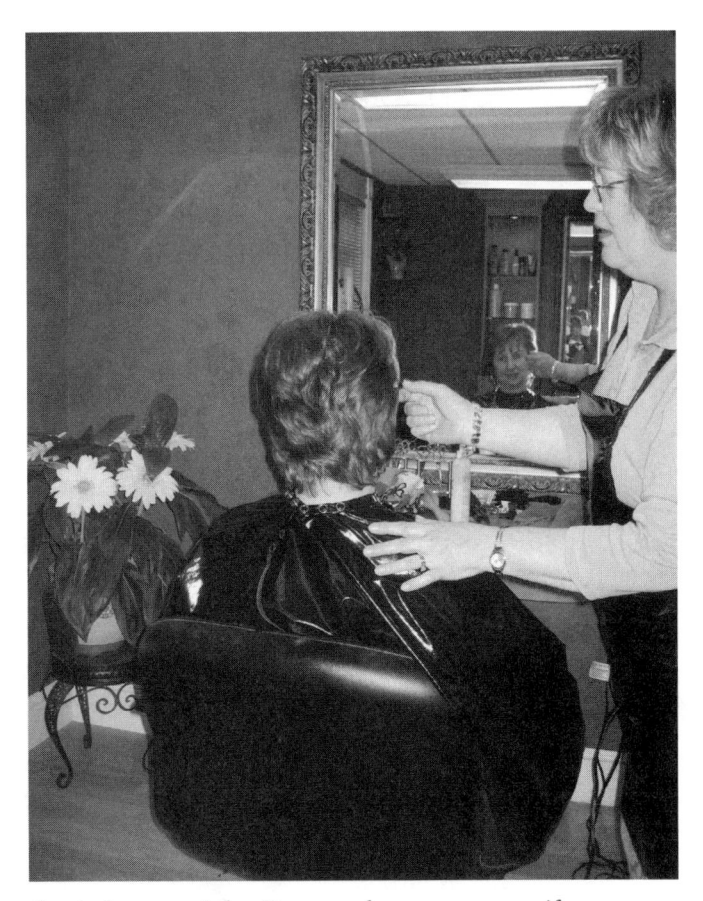

Sue is the pro at Salon Tuscany who pampers my wife on her frequent days of beauty. I think I shattered the relaxed atmosphere when I barged in to grab this shot... (Photo by Joe Paradis).

Two Cents, 9-02-04

A Day of Beauty

What topic is more alien to the average guy's mind than the need for his wife or significant other to spend a day pampering herself? For me personally, a trip to the barber shop is a major pampering event—it takes about twenty minutes. When my wife steps out for some self-pampering of her own, it can be a day-long marathon of hair, nails, massage . . . you name it. But in the end, who'd want it any other way? Gives me time to mow the lawn . . .

I recently stopped by a friend's house to help him with a few chores. It was rather quiet as he opened the door, which prompted my question. "Where's Kathy?"

He hesitated a second and with the gravest of deliveries informed me. "She's out. For a day of beauty."

I nodded with equal gravity, not knowing what the heck he was talking about.

He explained. "You know . . . a day of beauty. That's when she goes out 'to be attended to'. It could be a massage, to have her nails done, her hair cut. And no matter what it is, it always takes a day. A day of beauty. This one's her massage."

I understood then. I could identify with my wife's similar day of beauty at the hairdresser. She calls it her "cut and color." I, the one with all the words, simply call it her "dye job." She never was enamored of me using that terminology, especially when she would ask me to write her hair appointments on the calendar. "Joanne. Dye job, 7 P.M." I'd scribble. She doesn't ask me to do that anymore.

We two wizened men proceeded to ponder this phenomenon known as a day of beauty. It indeed seemed true to both of us that such a day provides some measure of soothing relaxation to our better halves. It also seemed true that we were just a tad poorer at the end of each of these sessions. Our hands went simultaneously to our chins, with that classic scratching gesture that men use as they ponder.

My wife once told me that her favorite relaxation—her ultimate day of beauty, I suppose—is a pedicure. That fascinating procedure involves soaking her feet in water, cutting her toenails, massaging her feet and calves, and—the *pièce de résistance*—applying the toenail polish. I tried explaining these soothing qualities to my friend. His initial reaction was similar to mine. Neither of us could imagine who in their right mind would enjoy doing such a job. Although no doubt soaking the feet first probably makes the task more tolerable.

I mentioned that additional touch of pedicure finesse that my wife loves—when the pedicurist places her hands in paraffin wax and then slides them inside warm mitts. All while classical music plays in the background and her feet receive the royal treatment. "Just like Madge," I said.

"Huh?" he inquired.

"Madge. Madge!" I exclaimed. "The lady with the carrot red hair in the old Palmolive commercials? She played the part of a manicurist who soaked her clients hands in dish detergent to soften them."

"Ah, yes. Madge. The industry's come a long way since then, hasn't it?" mused my friend. "Now a one dollar bottle of dish soap, good for a million soakings, has been replaced by a $50-per-hour specialist."

"With music," I quickly added.

"Of course," he said. "Of course. With music. No extra charge."

We had, by then, exhausted this heady topic of a day of beauty. I felt like rushing right out to his kitchen for a hot towel, to apply soothingly to my face. I thought I saw him eyeing the drawer where they keep their toenail clippers.

But then Kathy came floating through the doorway, a tired but rested look on her face. That massage had obviously left her very relaxed, as supple as a jellyfish.

"Day of beauty, huh?" I asked offhandedly.

She looked at me, a bit surprised, then glanced at my friend. He just shrugged. "Joanne has a similar ritual. No big secret."

"It was wonderful," she sighed. "Wonderful."

We nodded our heads in unison, as we pondered and scratched.

Finally, my friend broke the silence. "Kathy," he asked, "..do we have any paraffin wax?"

Two Cents, 9-16-04

The Junk Drawer

Every house has a junk drawer. Many have several. In our house, we have junk drawers, junk piles, junk corners-of-the-room. It's not all junk really—more like unofficial storage locations for "stuff" that seems to accumulate at its own rapid pace. Admit it, you have these too. If you haven't seen the dog or cat in a few days, I'd suggest looking in your junk drawer. You never know.

I'm convinced that the secret to a man's soul can easily be found right within his own home. In the recesses of a place so sacred, so hallowed, that no one but the most callous of burglars would dare venture.

Yes, I'm speaking of . . . the family junk drawer.

Ah, the junk drawer. That seemingly bottomless storage bin composed not so much of junk, as of items that have "nowhere else to go." Sort of an "Island of Misfit Toys" for everyday knick-knacks. You wouldn't, for example, find a shirt in most junk drawers—they usually have their own special closet. Nor would you find dishes or tools or food. They all have their own defined locations. Hopefully . . .

What you will find are items such as I discovered when deciding, after much introspection, to dump the contents of our favorite junk drawer onto the kitchen floor for closer inspection. Please bear with me as I reveal to you those treasures that define our family's soul.

Here's that bicycle pump I've been looking for, over the last six months. It's right next to an unopened pair of men's shoe laces—I haven't worn anything but loafers for the past ten years, so those must be for posterity. There's a charger for a cell phone that I believe we discarded three years ago. And a couple of caster cups—no wait, eleven of them. In various sizes and shapes. I wonder what's under the furniture legs now? There's a Halloween pin, several key chains, a camera strap. A cat collar and tag from Cat Stevens, our meanest cat ever, who died fifteen years ago. And don't we all remember this deck of playing cards, depicting the bad guys from Saddam Hussain's regime? Most with mustaches, most now dead or captured.

This is the original Paradis junk drawer. It's since been supplemented by several others, strategically located throughout the house. (Photo by Joe Paradis).

After—ouch—sifting through the pile of loose push pins, I've uncovered *The Audubon Field Guide to North American Birds*, 1985 edition. We were big on backyard bird watching then. I question why there's a night light in this drawer. Probably could be put to better use somewhere else. Here's a birthday card for my daughter that we bought last year and obviously forgot about. A bit of Americana lies resting here as well—a stars and stripes hair pin, a little heart-shaped flag ornament, a George Bush "W '04" bumper sticker.

Lots of lacrosse memorabilia—an "I Love Lacrosse" pin. A bumper sticker that reads "This Car Stops for Lacrosse Games." My son's lacrosse picture from fifth grade—he's a senior now. A couple of great window decals. One reads "Ask Not What Your Dad Can Do for You, But What You Can Do For Your Dad." Fat chance. The other reads "Honor Thy Father or Be Grounded." Fatter chance.

Here's a coupon for Pizza Hut that expired June 1, 2002. A set of sewing needles and a spool of thread. That old cow bell from Switzerland, a souvenir from my sister's honeymoon nineteen years ago. A lot more too—pictures galore, prayer cards, a Halls cough drop, cherry flavored. And my favorite—a heart-shaped welcome sign, painted on slate. No wonder the drawer was so heavy. I won't bore you with the other 43 items in this drawer—trust me, I've counted them.

The bottom line on all this? Well, I guess my family has a dusty soul. There obviously hasn't really been much added to this drawer in over two years. Which makes me suspicious ... maybe they've found some other drawer in which to squirrel away our valued treasures, those cherished pieces of loving nostalgia that define a family. I think I'll go looking for it. Just as soon as I throw away this pile of crap.

Two Cents, 9-23-04

Baseball Etiquette

When I watched my first Red Sox ballgame on a big screen TV, I was amazed at the clarity of the picture. It is so fine tuned that you can literally see the nose hairs on a pitcher as the camera zooms in on him—not that you'd want to, but they're there. You can also see the steady streams of saliva that every baseball player seems to spew out each time he's at the plate. I thought this deserved some attention, if only among my humble circle of readers and a whole bunch of parents raising future ballplayers.

If you've never done so, you really need to drop by a local ballpark to experience the emotions of small children as they learn the basics of the venerable game of baseball. Watch those six-year old boys, with T-shirts to their ankles, sporting baseball caps with the cheap plastic straps in the back. No matter how tightly you adjust those straps, the caps still swim on their heads.

You'll experience the complete sense of childish oblivion displayed by a seven-year old girl practicing her dance pirouettes in the outfield, as a fly ball sails over her head. She'll continue to dance until her dad reminds her to retrieve the ball and toss it to her shortstop. Or you may witness the joy of a five-year-old hitting the ball off a tee and running straight up the line—to third base.

But to really experience baseball, watch the patient coaches. Those who spend time teaching the kids baseball fundamentals—and the etiquette of our Great American Pastime.

Remember these experiences. Cherish them. Because "the realities of life" soon kick in for those kids good enough to continue with the sport and actually make a career of baseball. The intensity of the game changes. And the etiquette changes. Boy, does the etiquette change! Because, in addition to honing their baseball skills, young baseball players become experts at another art. The fine art of spitting.

I'm not sure at what point in a baseball player's training that the course on spitting is introduced. But they sure become good at it. You've seen professional players on TV. They'll sit in the dugout and spit. Not generally out on the field, however. No, no, no. They'll just drop a lung patty right at their feet. It's a wonder no one ever slips and breaks a leg. Or worse yet, drowns.

Watch them in the on-deck circle. They'll take a practice swing, then huck a lunger. Another swing. Another lunger. Endless cycle. Thank God the surrounding area is clay; otherwise they'd be wallowing in mud. And it makes you wonder why anyone would ever want to slide into first base—especially head first. I'm sure spit was the catalyst for the rule that allows a player to overrun first base.

I believe the truly best baseball expulsions, however, are reserved for the TV cameras. You've seen the classic camera pose. A player comes to the batter's box, taps his bat on the plate, launches into a few practice swings. Then he spews a bucketful of saliva down the line. And, of course, the *pièce de résistance* follows. He'll make . . . "the adjustment." If you have to ask . . . well, don't.

Baseball players spit a variety of substances as well. Many chew gum. Not just a stick, as you or I might, but something the size of a brick. And that brings out all the juices. Other players chew tobacco, which promotes a need to constantly spit. They'll munch on a wad as big as the bubble gum brick, but lumpier—more like a cud, with stray pieces protruding from the corners of their mouths. Players who chew tobacco are usually recognizable by the brown drool stains on the front of their uniforms. And they generally can't spit as far. I suppose the tobacco makes for a heavier lugie.

No other sport visibly promotes spitting the way baseball does. I've never seen a football player spit in a game. Hopefully, most of them are smart enough to know that spitting through the face guard of a football helmet isn't recommended. You don't see basketball players spitting on the court. They have enough of a challenge navigating their pools of sweat that savvy arena employees are constantly mopping off the court. And hockey players? They're too busy throwing checks and punches to think much about spitting, although I suspect they aren't just lacing up their skates when they bend down on the bench. Probably closet spitters.

Nonetheless, with these somewhat disturbing images firmly lodged in your mind, I still encourage you to visit a ball field and watch those little kids scamper down the base paths. And if you see one who appears to have a natural talent for the game, take his coach aside. And suggest that he invest in a roll of duct tape. Just to stave off the spitting habit as long as possible.

You were thinking maybe Manny Ramirez? Actually this is Miles Blackburn, my nephew from Chicago, who thankfully hasn't developed the spitting etiquette of professional ballplayers . . . not yet, anyhow. He does, however, occasionally spray you when he speaks. (Photo by Michael Blackburn).

No, these women aren't cutting through The Home Depot parking lot on their way home from the supermarket. They are actually a few of the many women who compete with guys at the hardware store on a daily basis. It's no longer a safe haven where guys can go to avoid washing the dishes. You're just as likely to run into your wife . . . or your mother-in-law. So you better shop wisely . . . (Photo by Joe Paradis).

Two Cents, 9-30-04

The Girls of Home Depot

I must admit that hardware stores are my favorite place to shop. You can have the malls, the shopping centers, the gift shops all to yourself, America. Give me a store where I can smell lumber and paint as soon as I step through the door and that's where I'll be shopping. I could spend all day in a hardware store, maybe not even buying anything, maybe just unwrapping a sandwich and sitting down on a pallet of garden loam for lunch. And as you'll see in this story, just watching the world go by.

Traditionally, hardware stores have been the venue of the American male. Manly places, with aisle after aisle of shiny tools, all types and sizes of lumber, plumbing and electrical supplies, and enough landscaping materials to keep a guy drooling for days. They've been a guy's home away from home, a respite from Saturday morning laundry, food shopping, and vacuuming the rugs.

I've always believed that some of that "guy only" stigma has faded. After all, women do many home repair projects these days, as well. And they must shop for those supplies. But I've never really observed them in action—and that bugged me. So I did what any self-respecting manly guy would do. I took a fieldtrip to Home Depot, honeyspot of the do-it-yourselfer. To see for myself whether there were, indeed, a few brave women who had struck out on their own to violate this stereotypical domain of the American male.

Truthfully, I was expecting to find strong, bruising women with rippling muscles, wearing faded jeans, steel-toed boots, and bandanas. Construction workers or electricians, pulling up in pickup trucks, with sleeves rolled up, hair pulled back, and dirt under the fingernails. Nice girls, of course—but not the kind to whom you'd give a tough time.

Boy, was I wrong. The first woman I observed was in the carpet department. She was leaning on her orange shopping cart, a cup of coffee in one hand, a store brochure in the other. Suddenly she spoke. "Honeeeeeey . . . ?" in a distinct cooing tone. I've seen that tactic used before and figured her husband had probably just scurried over three aisles.

I sought out other women. There were few venturing out alone. A middle-aged couple stood blocking the aisle of the lumber department. He was pulling out sheets of paneling, as she directed him. They seemed undecided about something, so they sat on a bench to consult a magazine she had been holding. They were obviously hot on the track of a home project. When their voices became heated, I figured it was my turn to scurry away.

Perhaps the person who most knew what she wanted at Home Depot was the five-year-old girl in the plumbing aisle. She ran up and down that aisle, lifting all the toilet seat covers one at a time, and letting them slam back down, each time with a giggle. Meantime, her mother was gazing at the mirrored medicine chests—more to fix her hair than select that all important storage unit.

And it may just have been family day at Home Depot that Saturday. One young mom was deciding on a lockset for the front door, as her young daughter hung over the side of her car-shaped shopping cart drawing imaginary circles on the floor. Another family, two kids in the cart, was agonizing through a decision on which caulking to buy for the tub. Really agonizing.

Then there were the women who came in, just tagging along behind their husbands. Some seemed to care, others didn't. A middle-aged guy, balding and with a dirty white ponytail, sauntered down the plumbing aisle. His wife followed closely behind, with a cartload of plumbing fixtures and an obvious look of boredom shrouding her face. Plumbing is not an exciting department. Except for that little girl who continued slamming the toilet seat covers ten feet away.

The paint department was a popular place for women that morning. One couple was fawning over the gallons of paint that people return because the color's just not what they wanted. These come at bargain prices for the next lucky buyer. "Fred, get that one. That one there. No, the green one. The GREEN one. I think it will match the bathroom," screeched his wife, who will probably return that gallon tomorrow. Or tell Fred to do it. I pitied Fred.

Surveying the girls of Home Depot would not be complete without recognizing those who work there. They were wonderful, guiding many a lost do-it-yourselfer through these aisles of the kingdom. One young lady was helping a fellow male employee set up a display table. He was having trouble unjamming a nail gun. So she nicely extracted the poor tool from his frustrated grip and tapped it twice against the table, whereupon . . . it worked. You go, girl!

But the woman of the day, in my mind, was the one who decided to brave the embarrassment of the self-service line. Where you scan your own purchases and hope you get out the door without the alarm going off because you missed an item. She'd scanned everything and was checking out when I happened upon her, but she just couldn't find the change return slot. She was speaking either to God or the machine, calmly saying "Okay now, I put the money in that slot, and it told me to look under the screen for my change. But where is it?" Since God speaks in mysterious ways and the machine wasn't about to answer, I showed her myself. An eternally grateful patron she was.

So that was my Saturday morning observation of the girls of Home Depot. And, sadly, I must conclude that its reputation as a bastion of the male stereotype still appears to be accurate. Perhaps next Saturday I'll hop down to the laundromat. Just to see how many guys are folding clothes.

Baseball's greatest rivalry—Yankees vs. Red Sox. I couldn't resist pulling out my Red Sox cap from the 2004 World Series and my Yankees cap from the 2001 World Series. Play ball! (Photo by Joe Paradis).

Two Cents, 10-28-04

If I Were a Yankees Fan . . .

I love New York. I truly do. The bustle of the city, the sights and sounds, the attitude. I love the raw, earthy atmosphere that surrounds just about every New Yorker I know. But alas, I was born and raised in Boston—and there we part ways. For I am a diehard Red Sox fan. And in the midst of the greatest sports rivalry in modern history, it's no big surprise that I chose to dis Yankees fans, after the Sox simply disgraced New York during the 2004 ALC playoffs when it came down to the wire (We won't discuss that Mets victory in 1986). Boston went on its way to win "our" first World Series in 86 years. We may never do it again, but for a diehard Red Sox fan like me, there's solace in knowing that at least once in my lifetime, we won it all. Now God and I will really have something to talk about when I get to the Pearly Gates. I'm told He's a Yankees fan.

It's easy to gloat when your team is winning. As a Red Sox fan, it's tempting for me to do that right now—particularly because we don't get that many chances to gloat. But I won't do it—and I don't believe many true Red Sox fans will either. Because we, of all sports fans, understand the exhilaration of watching our team claw its way to the top of the mountain, only to be pushed off the peak without a parachute.

I, for one, would instead like to offer my condolences (giggle) to Yankee fans everywhere for having to cope (tee hee hee) with a massive dual devastation. First, the Yankees made sports history by allowing (not that they had a choice) their opponent (that's us) to rally from a three-game deficit and crush them. Secondly, they suffered that most humiliating of defeats in their own home park, in the very House That Ruth Built.

So I would offer the following advice to Yankees fans.

If I were a Yankees fan, I would take consolation from the fact that my team has still won twenty-six World Series to Boston's four. Even though the 2004 ALCS results will stick in my throat forever, like a cancerous growth threatening to slowly choke the life out of me.

If I were a Yankees fan, I'd realize that the only TRUE Yankees fan is the one born in New York City. The true fan grows up with his hometown team like a family, living through the agony of the bad times and the thrill of the good times. All other so-called "fans" are fair-weather fans, who have never developed productive hobbies.

If I were a Yankees fan, I would disown Alex Rodriguez. He is not a true Yankee, just another high-paid superstar who thought that adding his talents to the perennial aura of the Yankees would automatically bring him the World Series ring he's never had. His little boy tactics in Game 6, swiping the ball out of Bronson Aroyo's glove, displayed his real "win at any cost" mentality. He's a cheater and a liar. And I've noticed, he is constantly picking his nose.

If I were a Yankees fan, I would not at all like the fact that an umpire making a piddling $400,000 a year has the power and authority to humble my baseball superstar who makes $18 million a year. That's like a minimum wage kid in a supermarket bossing around the president of General Electric.

If I were a Yankees fan, I would now understand that spending $186 million a year on players' salaries doesn't guarantee a winning team. The Red Sox proved it can be done with a mere $127 million. Even better, the Cardinals did it with $83 million. Of course, at the other end of the spectrum, the Milwaukee Brewers lost big this year, but only spent $27 million doing so. Did I mention the Yankees did that too—for $186 million?

If I were a Yankees fan, I would understand that, during this ALCS, Major League umpires took a huge leap forward in obtaining the respect of fans everywhere, because they were willing to confer with one another over questionable calls. We should all want to win fair and square, not because of an erroneous call by an umpire. Ain't that right, A-Rod?

If I were a Yankees fan, I would take comfort in knowing that George Steinbrenner will once again open up the checkbook this winter—maybe sooner—and hand out another chunk of change to a new crop of overpaid free agent superstars, in his annual attempt to buy a World Series. It's really irked him that the Yankees haven't won a series in four years . . . Red Sox fans are happy with one every 86 years.

If I were a Yankees fan, I would grin just a wee bit at the Yankees intentional dig at Boston in Game 7 in New York, when they let Bucky

Dent throw out the first pitch. But, of course, I'd still express my outrage that Boston would bring Pedro Martinez into that game for one inning, just to taunt the crowd. I'm not sure Pedro would tell you that that was his best outing . . .

If I were a Yankees fan, I would say I've had enough of Derek Jeter. Just as Nomar became an intense, unproductive burden to Boston, so too is Jeter becoming one to New York. Perhaps this winter, "Mr. Yankee" can sit down for a normal bowel movement and get back on the party circuit, surrounded by all those babes in his VISA commercial. Oh, I forgot—this year, he doesn't have to wait until the winter.

If I were a Yankees fan, I would perhaps concede that the most disciplined, well-groomed team that fears the wrath of its owner is not always the team that comes out on top. A real team can still play as a team, even with long hair and beards. As I recall, the Yankees teams of the 1970s looked like that. But then again, the Yankees weren't exactly winning in the '70s.

If I were a Yankees fan, since I'd always want to be the first to do everything, I'd start instituting a tradition of baseball teams shaking hands after a game. It's the only sport in which the winning team just indulges itself in celebrating a win, while ignoring the other team. Maybe the Yankees could start that tradition during their very next game . . . which is sometime in April 2005.

And finally, if I were a Yankees fan, I'd sit down on a curb somewhere, hang my head, and just cry my eyes out. Because, as Red Sox fans know, losing hurts. And coming so close and still losing hurts even worse. But as your daddy can tell you, two aspirins and a long winter will heal that pain.

So, Yankees fans, tell me . . . who's your daddy?

From the bleachers, Fenway Park doesn't look much different today than it did 40 years ago, when my brother Paul and I first discovered baseball. Except maybe for the price of a ticket. We paid fifty cents in 1966 to sit on any bench in the bleachers. Today we'd pay $25—but you get your own plastic seat and a cup holder. (Photo by Joe Paradis).

Two Cents, 11-04-04

Two Boys and a Game

There are three things in life that give me more pleasure than anything else... well, maybe four things, but we're only going to discuss three of them. Those three are rock n' roll, stamp collecting, and baseball. An interesting combination of hobbies, don't you think? Of the three, baseball was the last to catch my fancy. In 1966, I was laughed at for not knowing that Boston and San Francisco didn't play each other during the regular season (although today, with inter-league play, I'd be correct). But Carl Yastrzemski and The Red Sox Impossible Dream Team of 1967 provided my first real baseball education. And ever since then, I rarely miss a Red Sox game. Neither does my brother.

The two young boys first caught Red Sox Fever during the summer of 1967. Brothers from Arlington, Massachusetts, one was twelve years old and the other ten. For a half dozen weekends that magical summer, they would ride the bus to Harvard Square in Cambridge and switch to another bus to Mass. Ave. in Boston, a trip that no mother today would dare let her children take. They would then walk about a half mile to Fenway Park, the home of their heroes. Their ritual always included a stop on the corner of what is now Yawkey Way, to gaze up at the hallowed stadium where their idol Carl Yastrzemski played.

The twenty-cent bus fare depleted much of their savings, so they always sat in the bleachers, a fifty-cent bargain really, which included a guaranteed sunburn. They would buy lunch, a bag of peanuts, from the cart outside the park—those always tasted better than the pre-packaged ones sold inside Fenway. They remember once stacking the empty peanut shells, one at a time, on the hat brim of an old gentleman who sat in front of them. And laughing forever as all those shells fell into his lap when he lowered his head. Yes, the brothers were indeed young and a bit mischievous.

But they loved baseball and the Red Sox and, in the summer of the Impossible Dream, that's all that mattered. Their love of the game was not something nurtured from the time they could talk, as their dad was not a sports fan. In fact, their baseball curiosity had piqued only the year before, when the older boy had been embarrassed in school on a baseball question. Having overheard two schoolmates talking of baseball, he asked "Are the Red Sox playing the Dodgers this weekend?" His answer was greeted by a couple of blank stares, followed by laughter. From that moment on, he vowed to learn this game that almost everyone else seemed to instinctively know.

And learn the game he did, side-by-side with his younger brother. They would play catch on the six-foot-wide patch of grass next to their garage, taking turns being the pitcher and the catcher. They used garden knee pads as catcher's gear and a piece of shingle for the pitcher's mound. They were given new baseball gloves by a character named Tony, who frequented the Rose Wharf area of Boston Harbor where their father ran a lobster shack. A nice guy, that Tony, but not one whom you'd dare ask "where did you get those gloves?"

The boys fantasized the summer away and were in their glory when Yastrzemski and Jim Lonborg led their beloved Sox into the World Series, a first in their young lives—in the lives of many for that matter. Although heartbroken by the Sox' hard-fought defeat in that Fall Classic, the boys went on to love the game even more, buoyed by meeting Red Sox players Ken Harrelson, Gary Bell, and Joe Foy the next year.

They continued to ride the Red Sox roller coaster for the next 37 years.

1975 was a dream year once again for the Sox, as they battled the Cincinnati Reds in the World Series. Although the brothers had gone down separate life paths by then, they continued to share their love of the Sox and the hope of a World Series Championship. When Carlton Fisk made baseball history in Game 6 of that World Series, the older boy was listening at 4 a.m. from an Air Force base in Korea. His howls of joy woke the few guys in the barracks who weren't themselves listening to the game on tiny transistor radios, while shivering in their cots. Meanwhile, his brother was enjoying the same game 12,000 miles away, with a group of friends in a Boston tavern. Despite the miles between them, they both pouted for days after Game 7 that year.

They survived the "Series Win That Almost Was" in 1986, no doubt losing years off their lives, as did many Red Sox fans, when that ball dribbled between Bill Buckner's ailing legs into right field. Superstars like Fred Lynn, Jim Rice, Wade Boggs, and Roger Clemens weren't enough to trump the Mets and alter the course of fate. But the brothers, by now raising their families in separate states, talked of the heartbreak, and decided to focus on the Celtics who were having their own second dynasty. It somehow eased the pain.

They agonized through the promising years of the 1990s, when the leadership of Mo Vaughn, Mike Greenwell, and Roger Clemens brought so much hope to Red Sox fans, still hurting from that World Series debacle of just a few years earlier. Yet, it wasn't meant to be for the Sox that decade, as first Cleveland and then the Yankees blocked their way to the Fall Classic throughout the 1990s. The brothers continued with their family lives, disappointed by the letdown, but becoming involved in their own kids' introductions to the world of sports.

By the time of the new millennium, the brothers had settled into that mid-life portion of their lives, one of them graying, the other balding. One had survived his kids' teenage years; the other was just entering that phase. And they had pretty much resigned themselves to the fact that the Yankees would always be a perennial impediment to their beloved Sox ever reaching another World Series.

But God takes pity on the weak and, at long last, the boys are at peace with their Red Sox, who overcame tremendous odds and the hardy skepticism of their fans, ingrained from so many years of denial, to finally win a World Series this year. Each is happy, gratified even, to know that their prayers have been answered—the Red Sox have won it all for once—and during their lifetime.

The team that they have worshipped for nearly 40 years is no longer just Boston's or New England's team. The Red Sox are now a Nation, and rumor has it, they have become "America's Team." But to the two brothers, the Sox will always be the hometown team. The team that two little boys used to visit so many years ago on those hot summer afternoons. When peanut shells on an old man's hat brim were the funniest thing going. And the pressures of grinding through year after year of "almost making it" and praying for one—just one—World Championship weren't part of the equation.

The Paradis brothers can now die happy. Well, we'd like a few more years first, of course. And maybe, just maybe . . . one more World Series Championship???

Reed Paige Clark, III and his charming wife Phyllis live in the family farmhouse in Londonderry NH, built by Reed's ancestors in 1839. Reed has been my biggest proponent of redefining "the elderly" as "the enlightened" at every opportunity, although truthfully, we really don't see the new term catching on. And I'm not sure, but I think Phyllis still calls him' the old guy' anyhow ... (Photo by Joe Paradis).

Two Cents, 11-18-04

Redefining the Golden Years

Reed Paige Clark is a dear friend of mine. We have a lot in common. We attend the same church, are involved in local volunteer efforts, and share a mutual interest in how our town is governed. The only real gap we have between us is age. Reed is seventy-something and I am fifty-something. That's never been a problem, but whenever Reed spoke about his generation, he referred to them as "seniors" or "the elderly." He doesn't anymore. We've come up with a new phrase now. Read on, Reed.

Listen up now, all of you from the "Greatest Generation." We've gotta talk. I'm having a problem with terminology these days. As I get closer to my golden years, I'm not so sure that I want to be known as a "senior citizen" or "the elderly" or an "old timer." None of those phrases quite defines what you really are when you've reached the height of wisdom and have nothing more to prove. Wouldn't you agree?

What's a "senior citizen" anyhow? How do you differentiate one from a junior citizen? Is it more time in grade? Should there be freshmen and sophomore citizens as well? In Spanish, Signor Citizen would mean Mr. Citizen. Does that make any sense? It certainly leaves Mrs. Citizen out of the definition. No, I don't think I want to be known as a senior citizen. Too patronizing.

What about "the elderly"? Puleez... Why not just say "the declining," which the thesaurus lists as a synonym for elderly? Or we could reference Webster's dictionary, where the definitions aren't any more flattering. "One who lived at an earlier period." Correct me if I'm wrong, but aren't "the elderly" still alive? Or how about these definitions—"somewhat old," "rather advanced in years," or "somewhat past middle age." Talk about political correctness. Let's just lay it out straight, Mr. Webster! Why not call 'em "old as dirt"? No, I don't want to be known as "the elderly" either—or even some refinement of the term, like "elder statesman." That would remind me of the Senate in ancient Rome. And that's way too old.

I wouldn't be keen on being called an "old-timer" either. That's something you'd hear Eddie Haskel call his grandfather in an old "Leave It To Beaver" rerun. Why not just say "old geezer" or "old fart"? Or keep the old out of it and just call 'em "antique" or "obsolete." No, none of those terms will do. I don't want to be known as an "old timer"—or anything like it.

No, there needs to be a term that better defines those who've reached the "golden years"—and there's yet another term that needs redefinition. Otherwise, I guess I'm in my "silver years" now. Which probably puts my kids in their "bronze years" or some other year of a less valued metal.

What we need is a term that defines the essence of wisdom, the pinnacle of practical thought, the epitome of a life well lived and lessons long ago learned. How about "The Mature"? Doesn't really work for me personally—I doubt that, even in my advanced years, I'd ever be mistaken for mature. But some might like that.

How about "The Wizened"? Naw. Reminds me a bit too much of an owl sitting in a tree, head swiveling back and forth as he looks for field mice. Or perhaps of an old medicine man in the middle of Africa, who knows, from memory, the history of his village going back 10,000 years. That's a neat talent, but most of us, even at my age, often can't remember why we went down the cellar stairs a minute ago without retracing our steps to rekindle the thought. Forget 10,000 years of family history.

But wait . . . I think I've got it. The perfect word for "people-older-than-I-by-at-least-fifteen-years." A word that defines all that you bring to the table of life; that captures the essence of your full comprehension of worldly things. The one term that gives you the right to laugh out loud at the absurdity and stupidity that dribbles from the mouths of those younger than you.

Let's call you . . . "The Enlightened." Yeah, I like that. "The Enlightened." No more "senior citizen" or "elderly" or "old timer." Just . . . "The Enlightened." I picture an almost angelic figure in a white robe. Standing on a cloud, arms outstretched, with beams of light radiating from behind. Maybe a halo.

No more Grandpa or Grandma. It would be "Oh Enlightened One." All-knowing. In an earthly sense, of course.

What think ye, Town Elders?

Two Cents, 12-30-04

The Family Christmas Letter

I don't really know why, but few things get my goat more than those family letters that some folks send out at Christmas time, in lieu of a greeting card. They either contain sickly sweet language about how wonderfully their perfect, little cherubs are growing up or they provide pretty detailed descriptions of dad's gastric bypass surgery or Auntie Mary's impending death. Not the stuff you really want to hear during the Season of Joy. So I thought I'd concoct a little spoof on the family Christmas letter, totally fabricated and with all apologies to any family that might actually have the name Gastronimi...

Before we let another Christmas season settle into the mythical snow bank, I'd like to take a shot at one of my biggest pet peeves—those family letters that some people stuff into their Christmas cards. You know, the letter that tells you everything about their family. How perfect the kids are. How big the house is. How wonderful the job is. How many social events they've been to in the past year. Who's sick; who died. I've had to run for the toilet after reading some of these, with an urge to purge. Pleeez...

So in the spirit of this phenomenon, I present to you my spoof of:

The Gastronimi Family Christmas Letter

Happy Holidays to all our friends and family from the Gastronimis! This is our thirteenth annual letter and we hope you've enjoyed every one of them. I know we have. Where should we start this year?

The kids are all doing great. Reba just turned twelve and is doing well in the halfway house. Reform school was a bit tough for her, but she seems to have conquered the urge to turn all the outside faucets on throughout the neighborhood. We admit that last flood wasn't pretty and we all really miss Mr. Kiley's dog.

Keep those Christmas cards comin'! Just leave the sordid family details at home, will ya? No one cares about your bunion operation . . . (Photo by Joe Paradis).

Leviticus continues to build his spiked dog collar collection. He has over sixty of them now and tries to wear a different one each day. We have to admit he goes through a lot of collared shirts, but luckily, everything he wears is black, so it's hard to notice the shreds. He has a new haircut too—he'll single-handedly bring back the Mohawk, our little fashion freak!

Moon Unit, our youngest, is starting to use the toilet now. She was having some difficulty telling the difference between the cat's litter box and the toilet, but we think that's been resolved. We expect the cats to return any day.

Nancy has just taken the Bar Exam for the ninth time. We're very excited! She's hopeful this might be the last, but is seriously considering other options, just in case. She's somewhat intrigued by public service and thinks being a meter maid might be fun. Or making pottery. Either way, she still plans to save time to grow her Jerusalem artichokes and hunt turtles. She still enjoys collecting old tires and has over 500 in the garage. Someday she'll get around to sorting them by size and manufacturer, maybe when the kids finally graduate from school in fourteen or fifteen years.

Jeff's business continues to grow. His patent for the dung beetle lure was just approved and he thinks this could be our big financial breakthrough. At least we might be able to get the station wagon back after Mr. Spigattoni's friends came to take it away. Jeff's legs are starting to heal nicely too.

Family trips this year included a ride to Hooksett to visit the new Shaw's, a family walk behind the shed to see what really lives there, and a quick visit to the neighbors' pool while they were shopping last summer. Moon Unit hurt herself climbing out of the pool and we're thinking of filing a lawsuit. People shouldn't put jelly fish in their pool where others could get hurt.

We also visited Uncle Ned at "The Big House." He's doing just fine and expects to be out in ten or twelve years, with good behavior—or sooner, he says. We brought him those brochures about South American countries, like he asked. Gramps and Nanny bring him a loaf of bread every day and he always brags to us about his great file and hacksaw blade collection. Everyone in our family collects something!

We close with gratitude to all of you, our friends and family, especially to Larry for putting out that little fire and to cousin Frank for the used sweatbands. Sincere wishes for a wonderful holiday season and a healthy new year.

The Gastronimi Family

JEFF   *Nancy*   *Reba*

Leviticus   *moon Unit*

Large gatherings with friends or family at a restaurant can be fun. But it's probably a good idea to work out the payment arrangements beforehand—and leave the weapons at home . . . like these deck officers do when they break bread aboard a U.S. Navy destroyer. (Photo by Robert Paradis).

Two Cents, 2-24-05

Splitting the Bill

I have received more comments on this article than on just about anything I've written in my column. I thought my wife's family was the only one that actually partook of these ritual family gatherings, usually at less expensive restaurants with good food. But apparently not. Those restaurants seem to understand the give and take of large families bartering over who ate what. They know that, in the end, the tip will be a good one—to apologize for disturbing the other patrons.

It's probably an American ritual. A right of passage that we pass along to our children. The hallowed event at a fancy restaurant, when the whole family gathers. We eat forever and drink a little wine. And reminisce and enjoy one another's company.

Until the bill comes—this one for $265.00. Then all bets are off. The gloves are dropped and the calculators come out.

"Who had the veal parmigiana?" offers Uncle Ted, the accountant. The posturing begins.

"Which one, the special or the regular one?"

"Does it matter?"

"Well, yeah. The special was $2.00 more. Didn't you have that one, Freddy?"

"I don't know. Jean ordered for me. I was in the Men's Room."

"Who had the clam chowder? There are six of them on the bill." Everyone looks at one another. No one remembers.

"I think I had a salad," offers sister Pat. "But it came with my meal. I think."

"Well, I figured ours out already. Jim and I owe $14."

"Didn't you guys have the Prime Rib?" questions Aunt Mary. "And four drinks?"

"Did you figure in the tip? And that 8% meals tax?"

"Well, we're not paying for something we didn't eat."

"What about your kids? The four of them ate off the regular menu. Our kids just had the hot dogs."

Tempers begin to heat up, almost as quickly as his calculator keypad, as Uncle Ted tries feverishly to make some sense of this mess. Precious minutes tick away. Grandma's flatulence is easily detected in the quiet that envelops the room.

"Let's just each chip in the same amount," offers Cousin Tony. "Then it's a square deal."

"That's easy for you to say," bellows Uncle Ross from across the table. "That wife of yours ate enough for four." That stops Tony's wife dead in her tracks. She licks the rest of the whipped cream off Grandma's spoon and begins to bristle. It's getting personal now. The quiet turns into the confusion of eighteen voices talking over one another.

"Calm down everyone," yells Grandpa, face reddening brightly. The last time he looked like that, he had a stroke, thinks Grandma to herself. She reels off a silent prayer. "We've gotta get through this," he says. "So everyone shut up. Gimme the bill," he says to Uncle Ted, who mops his brow and slouches back in his chair, relieved to have the pressure taken off him.

"I'm sending this around the table," Grandpa instructs them. "Put your name next to everything your family ate. Don't cheat or I'll take you out of my will."

And the orderly progression of the bill begins, passed from one chair to the next. Down the left side of the table, up the right side. Neat little names printed next to each meal. Except for Uncle Gustave, who can't write. But everyone knows the 'X' next to the meatloaf is his.

Five minutes later, the bill returns to Grandpa. "Thank you," he says sternly. "Now, Ted, add up what each of us owes. And tack on the tax and a 20% tip."

A few peeps are emitted at the mention of the tip rate. Shirley elbows her husband. "The will," she whispers. "Remember the will."

Uncle Ted puts his CPA degree to good use. He comes up with the figures in less than five minutes. The deed is done. The figures announced. The money silently emerges from wallets and purses and is placed on top of the bill. Everyone, of course brought twenty dollar bills, but no one dares to ask for change. The waitress really makes out on this deal. She earned every penny of it, with this bunch.

"Now go home," says Grandpa, as he helps Grandma out of her chair, nose wrinkling slightly from the remnants of her flatulence. "And thanks for the birthday dinner."

Perhaps some family rituals should be revised.

It's a scary thought—communicating without even opening your mouth. But kids these days have mastered it, thanks to such technology as Instant Messaging and texting. This generation may lose the ability to interact verbally, but they sure are becoming fast typists . . . (Photo by Joe Paradis).

Two Cents, 3-03-05

I M, I Said

(with apologies to Neil Diamond)

I am a frequent user of e-mail and the internet. Couldn't live without the tool—and that's what I consider it, merely a tool. I contact whomever I want or research some information I need, and boom . . . I'm off that computer and on to other things. But kids these days—to them, life IS the computer. And IM-ing one another, whether through MySpace or any of the other chat room vehicles, is how they seem to communicate. God forbid they pick up the phone and actually talk. Why do that, when you can just send a text message? But this new distant method of communicating brings with it a new language and its uniqueness is what I tried to bring out in this little story.

There I was on-line last night, just minding my own business, answering a few million e-mails, when suddenly up pops this little box on my screen. "Hi," it said.

I shot a glance around the room. "*Aliens,*" I thought to myself. "*They're invading us through the Internet . . . we're doomed.*" Then I looked back at my computer screen and recognized the screen name next to the 'Hi'. It belonged to one of our interns at the newspaper. This type of communication had only happened one other time in my life, so I was excited. I typed back. "My, God. I've been IM'd!"

Her reply came back. "Sorry?"

I knew I'd lost her right there.

And that appears to be the rub with IM—or Instant Messaging, as the uninitiated, like myself, call it. You can't speak normally or type normally. You have to use some kind of code to be understood by the myriad of experienced telecommunicators on the net, admittedly many of the teenage variety.

I would occasionally watch my own daughter IM-ing away on the keyboard, trying to understand how this form of communication worked. She'd be typing at warp speed and I'd think to myself, "Wow, that kid can really type! At least she's building a useful skill for her future." Then I glanced at the screen, and read "oic. jk. u r kool. lol. bbl."

I figured maybe she just had her fingers on the wrong keys. So I worked up the nerve to ask. You know that rolling of the eyes and shaking of the head that kids give you when you ask them a stupid question? Well, I got that treatment. But she explained anyhow. Her jargon meant 'Oh, I see. Just kidding. You're cool. I'm laughing out loud. Be back later.' She typed in one more phrase—"h/o." That meant 'hold on'. Then she turned in her chair to provide dear old dad with insightful commentary and analysis.

"We can't type like you guys when we IM," she patiently related. "We don't use commas or periods or stuff that we would normally use in a writing class. We have to be quick."

I understood that part. My daughter is among a group of kids who will just go online and wait, sometimes for hours, until someone else comes on. They'll play solitaire or on-line games in the meantime, gearing their ears for that little jingling sound that indicates a friend has found them on-line. And inevitably six more friends pop on almost immediately. Then the heavy conversation begins. Two start; the rest listen.

"wats ^?"
"nm u?"
"nm r u goin 2 the dance?"
"ya"
"with chris?"
"ya"
"kool"
"u?"
"I dunno maybe chuck"
"lol"
"y?"
"hes a jerk"
"w/e"
"sorry"

By this time, three of the listeners become bored and pop off, as indicated by that neat little sound of a slamming door. Everyone has his or her own limits. Some will cycle back later. Others will go watch TV or cut their toenails or watch the grass grow. It's a whole new world of . . . conversation. Pop in, pop out.

Now these are some pretty intelligent kids. How this can go on for hours, I'll never know. But I believe I finally understand the concept . . . I think. Teenage IM-ing is just like two kids on the telephone. All that a well-intentioned, eavesdropping parent hears is one side of the telephone conversation—essentially a bunch of single words that mean nothing to the casual listener. In the IM world, kids just transfer this stimulating type of conversation to the computer screen. And it still appears to mean nothing—except to them.

I don't think many kids are discussing evolution or rehashing the Pythagorean theorem or conducting a book review when they IM. I think they're just having fun, chatting and being with one another. Sort of like when we used to hang out on the street corner as kids, until the bullies chased us away.

So I'm "kool" with this IM stuff. It makes me "lol," but that's "aight."

"ttyl."

(For translations, please consult your IM/English dictionary—on line, of course.)

To my mind, Jim Lockwood, a sports writer for The Londonderry Times, *is the model of manly selective hearing—and he's not even married yet. I see a bright future for him. (Photo by Joe Paradis).*

Two Cents, 3-03-05

Selective Hearing

Few things can anger a young wife more than being ignored, especially by her husband. After all, good marriages are based on trust and sharing. So naturally, a young wife expects her husband to listen to every word she says. And he'd better listen—or there's that couch he can always sleep on. However, as we age, gracefully or not, it isn't uncommon for the husband to obtain "selective hearing-osis," a condition that, after many years, even his wife accepts. By that time in their relationship, a stint on the couch—if even necessary—may even be a welcomed relief for both of them. So listen up to this story...

I find, as I get older, that my mind likes to compartmentalize things. This helps me to focus, I suppose, on the things that require particular concentration. I'm proud of that ability; it assists me in avoiding brain overload by tuning out peripheral thoughts.

I, like many guys, call this "selective hearing."

My wife calls it "not paying attention."

Either way, it's a real talent.

I've seen this trait in a lot of other men. Proud men, nearly always in their fifties or older. Men who've spent a lifetime grooming themselves for that perfect time—when they are finally asked a question that they just want to tune out. They usually test this God-given trait first with the response to a simple question, usually a trash-related one. It's nearly always a question asked by their wives, during the ninth inning of a Red Sox game. With the bases loaded, two outs, a full count, and David Ortiz at the plate.

"Honey, would you take the **ash out? It's pretty full and I'm afraid the dog will get into it."

Her husband's mind freezes. The eyes flicker, but his head doesn't turn. *Focus on the game,* his mind tells him. *On the game. I think she asked you about a gash. Or a rash. Yeah, that's it—a rash. Just watch the game.*

But his wife persists, ever so nicely. She's seen this trait in her own father. Momma said there'd eventually be days like this for her too. "Would you do that, please? Honey?"

"Sure," responds her husband. And after a slight delay, he adds "Do what?" Ortiz was bearing down at the plate, eyeing the opposing pitcher with that steady gaze of his.

"Take out the **ash," repeats his wife, now more certain than ever that her husband has entered the "place-where-all-men-eventually-go," the Land of Selective Hearing.

"But I don't have a rash," he shoots back, innocently. Ortiz had just swung through the final pitch. A big fat Strike Three. This game would go into extra innings. Dejected, her husband rises from his chair and heads for the trashcan. She can only shake her head.

It's a typical scenario played out time and again in households across the country; around the world even.

Now there are several variants of selective hearing. There's that general response that a guy provides when he's just plain tired. Instead of trying to decipher what his wife says to him, from the few words his ear picks up, he'll often just say "Huh?" It's a response that ensures continued conversation. Who can resist the urge to respond to a 'huh?'?. Huh? It actually clears the air, allowing a man's wife to repeat the question, perhaps more slowly. Rumor has it that Winston Churchill gave some of his most rousing speeches, throughout his lifetime, after a series of 'huhs?'. Homer Simpson too.

A guy with hearing aids can get away with utilizing selective hearing to a greater degree than those without hearing aids. He can just smile, nod his head, and cup a hand over the ear until his hearing aid emits that high pitched feedback whistle, which doesn't bother him, but startles everyone around him. A follow-up question usually isn't asked by the inquirer, fearing she's embarrassed the poor guy. It's a nifty ploy.

History might certainly have been different if more men had practiced the art of selective hearing down through the ages. French peasants might have heard Marie Antoinette exclaim "Let them eat steak," thereby diverting the French Revolution. General McArthur might have left the Philippines with a mere "Huh?" instead of "I shall return." And Richard Nixon might have been heard to exclaim "I'm not a schnook," proving only that he was still lying.

Yes, the fine art of selective hearing. Something for which young boys get spanked, but older men garner respect and sympathy. One of the many rewards of growing older, wouldn't you say? Huh?

It would have been tempting to lay out all of my tools for this picture. But I didn't have that kind of time . . . and I probably would have injured myself anyhow. (Photo by Joe Paradis).

Two Cents, 3-21-05

Collecting Manly Things

I'm not a "neanderthal" type of guy at all. I don't own the biggest truck on the block. I don't have a gun collection that mirrors that of the National Guard. I don't even have a wet bar in my basement with a built-in beer dispenser. But I do have lots of tools and I love to putter, so I collect whichever tools I need to undertake my "projects." Kind of like Tim "The Tool Man" Taylor. But collecting can get out of hand, something to which this article will attest...

When I was a child, collecting was a matter of patience and persistence. Mothers would collect S&H Green Stamps for years in order to save enough to cash in for an electric can opener. Today, S&H is out of business and you can pick up an electric can opener anywhere for $5.99.

Kids would buy and trade baseball cards for half their lives and still never collect the entire Red Sox series. Today, you can walk into WalMart and purchase a complete set of baseball cards, every team in the Major Leagues, for about $40.00.

You can now even purchase the entire collection of uncirculated U.S states commemorative quarters for a fee "slightly above cost." And half of them haven't even been minted yet! Yes, collecting has, indeed, become a lost art. With the convenience of purchasing an entire set of almost anything, the fun of collecting is essentially gone.

But there's at least one collection you can't buy right off the rack these days. Probably a good idea too, as many families would go broke.

That sacred collection is a man's tools. That hallowed conglomeration of work implements that some of us lovingly shine after each use, while others more nonchalantly toss them on the workbench until needed again. Ooh rah. I treasure my tools—I'm not at the point of sleeping with them, but do treat them like close friends.

A man's tool collection usually begins with the basics. I received my first tool kit as a small boy, the typical plastic hammer, saw, and screwdriver. They were fun implements for my brother and I to toss at each other and pretend we were sawing the legs off the dining room table. A few years after that, my parents took a huge step and bought me another set of kid's tools—miniature versions of a hammer, saw, pliers, and screwdriver made of real metal. Wisely, they didn't extend the same privilege to my brother, who had visions of tearing the house down and rebuilding from scratch. But these metal tools were the ultimate to my seven-year old mind (basically, the same mind I use today). I would take scrap pieces of wood that my Dad always saved, steal a few of his nails, and just hammer them into the wood. Then I'd stand back and admire my handiwork, sometimes for hours. I was indeed a carpenter genius.

Throughout my teenage years, I collected the usual assortment of tools, cheap things from Woolworth's, manufactured in Japan—when the Japanese still made crap—and sold under Woolworth's famed Homelife brand, another term for "junk."

In my 15th year, as the first hairs began to appear on my chin, I went all out and bought a Black & Decker drill. I'd saved all my pennies for that little baby. It was actually made of metal parts, something you won't find much today. It has been my constant companion for 35 years and finally died of old age just last year. I'm contemplating a burial plot out in the yard, in the pet cemetery. Words can't explain...

In subsequent years, I bought dozens of other manly tools. My first ChannelLock pliers when I was in electrical school—those babies can make a man drool. I actually cried when I lost them—and again when I found them in the back yard after the snow melted one winter. Don't ask...

My first circular saw was a pride and joy. I became enamored of this gem after watching my Dad zip his right through its electric cord. He put electrical service to the whole neighborhood out for 24 hours. Manly. I confined my blade to wood only.

The jig saw came next. Then another drill. A sander. A router, which to this day, I can't figure out. A table that turned my circular saw into a table saw—a Mickey Mouse contraption, but I felt like one of the big boys with that. The band saw was a great prize. We broke every rule in the Cub Scout manual, by helping our scouts make wooden airplanes with that cool tool. No fingers were lost, but I'll probably be thrown in jail now, after that confession.

In later years, when I could more readily afford some of the real "drool tools," I finally broke down and bought the ultimate machine—

a Saws-All. This baby cuts through anything. Anything... Had my brother had one of these when we were kids, his dream of tearing down the house could have come true in a day.

I've collected other standards of the manly tool crib too. The plumber's propane torch. A real table saw. An electric grinder. I finally even bought my own sledge hammer and pick, for those days when I just feel like throwing my back out.

And last week, I went whole hog. I bought a chain saw. Yeah, it has a lot of plastic in it, but that's how they make 'em these days. I'd tossed that purchase around for years, but could never really justify it. Always too easy to borrow one from a neighbor. You know how they're always out there saying things like "Mornin', Joe! Need to borrow my chain saw today?" So I bit the bullet. I did fell two trees before the chain loosened and came off. And I've spent more time tuning it that using it. But I think we're getting there. Although now I know why I waited so long to buy one.

I now believe though, that, for the average Joe, I probably have all the tools I need until they lock me away in the nursing home. Except perhaps for one more thing. A jackhammer... now, that's a real manly tool. I once used one during a summer job years ago and my muscles vibrated for a week afterward.

But, we'll see. You can only go so far with this collection thing before you get carried away...

Lots of guys can haul a new washing machine home from the store. But ask most of us how to actually use one, and you'll see how useless we really are in the area of domestic engineering. (Photo by Joe Paradis).

Two Cents, 5-19-05

Domestic Chores for the Man

In an age when both parents in most households work, it's interesting to observe how they handle the household chores. After all, just a generation ago, when I was growing up, my mother stayed home and took care of her four kids. The only thing she needed my father to do was drive her to the supermarket once a week. Otherwise, she had everything under control. But these days? Well, here's an example of daily life in the modern family . . . of course, from a guy's perspective.

It's a known fact that the male of our species falls way short of expectations in the area of domestic engineering. To put it more bluntly, we don't generally do much in the way of household chores—at least in the eyes of our wives. Oh sure, we mow the lawn, wash the car, and change the oil. We fix squeaky doors, leaky toilets, and broken computers. We assemble gas grills, cheap furniture, and every Christmas toy imaginable. We also paint the house, shingle the roof, rake the leaves, plant the garden, chop down trees, lug the trash out, and a few other things.

But we are acknowledged losers when it comes to those chores related to daily living—particularly in the areas of food, clothing, and dishes. I can bear witness.

There was a time when I was the one who did the food shopping. I'd take our list to Shaw's Supermarket each week and faithfully comb the aisles. I knew where everything was and could get out of there in less than an hour. The trick was to buy only what was on the list—straying always costs you time and money.

Today, I'm lucky if there's ever enough room on the shopping list to write in my few humble requests. My wife and daughter now do the shopping every Sunday after church, bringing home items I've never heard of. With two growing kids, one a veritable eating machine, our weekly food bill has jumped from $50 to $200 per week. I long for the days when I was able to sneak the Shaw's brand cereals past them—before they could read.

I have also been chastised by the House Police for doing a poor job with the laundry. I know enough to separate the whites from the darks—did that for years. And I've even reluctantly begun to separate the reds into their own pile. In my mind, red is a dark color, so I've always put those in the washer with the dark clothes. But Section 1.5A of the Domestic Laundering Manual apparently says no. Reds deserve their own space—and I'm cool with that.

But I'm confused as to why we need to separate the kids' jeans from everything else, hang them up to dry, and THEN put them into the dryer. What's the use in that? My clothes don't get such special treatment. And I don't know why certain of my wife's clothes need to go in cold water only, why my daughter's shirts each need "special attention," and why death is imminent if my son's clothes ever enter the dryer. So I confine my laundry chores to lugging the clothes baskets from the hamper to the laundry room.

Washing dishes may be foreign to most guys—and even many women, because the order of the day for cleaning dishes is to use the dishwasher. We have one of those, but it runs more water across the floor than through the wash cycle. So we wash dishes the old fashioned way.

And this is an area where I can do no wrong. I have free reign to wash all the dishes I'd like. Unlike food shopping, where everyone wants to make sure that their favorite foods are purchased, and clothes washing, where everyone wants to ensure that their favorite clothes aren't shrunk in half, nobody seems to care about a dish-free sink—except me. It's probably the only "neat freak" trait I inherited from my mother.

Given all the chores above that most guys can do correctly, it's nice to know we can take a breather on some of these others. But for my money, there's nothing like running my hands under hot water while scraping remnants of Hamburger Helper from the frying pan. Soothes the savage beast in me—before I have to go tackle a squeaky door.

Two Cents, 6-02-05

The Remote

Few things are nearer and dearer to our society these days than the television. But heaven forbid that, in a world of over 200 cable channels, we should ever have to rise from the couch to change channels. That was fine when we only had three channels to cope with, as I did growing up. But not now. And so we deal with "the remote." Some of us deal with three or four of them to control the HD TV, the DVD, and everything else that we squeeze into our "entertainment systems." And so, for couch potatoes everywhere, I present my tribute to the humble remote control.

Let's face it, there are certain species that just don't like to be found. A kid playing outside, who doesn't want to come in when his mother calls him. A cat that's finally been let out after a week of rain—you know what her attitude is. Or those car keys that you swear you put on the kitchen counter an hour ago. It's not that they're lost, mind you; it's merely that they don't want to be found. And the biggest violator of them all is any remote control device you might own. Any one of them. Turn your head the slightest bit and they're gone. As if they had legs . . .

The most common of these is, of course, the humble television remote. Generally black in color, these little buggers know they can blend in with their surroundings—and they know that drives you wild. It's not as if you don't treat them well. You feed them fresh batteries when they need them and lovingly wipe the goo from their buttons after your kid's peanut butter sandwich lands face down on it. In our house, we even provide shelter to our TV remote—a little pouch that hangs over the arm of the sofa. A nice cozy sleeping bag for this mechanical device that loves to please.

But for some reason, the slippery little thief likes to hop out of its pouch at the most god-forsaken times. Such as when my wife sits down to watch the final episode of "American Idol"—a travesty, in itself. Or if I want to hurriedly turn on a Red Sox game when the score is tied 9-9 in the top of the ninth (or desperately turn the game off when

Remote controls? We've got a dozen of them in our house, controlling everything from the TV and the DVD player to the air conditioner and even our automatic car starters. But it takes four of them to control the high definition television, because I refuse to spring $400 more for an all-in-one remote. (Photo by Joe Paradis).

they're losing 12-1 in the second). There then ensues a frantic search for the little guy—on the couch, the kitchen table, the Lazyboy. The search often goes deeper—to the guinea pig cage, the kitchen sink, the refrigerator, the toilet bowl. And just when we're about to give up, it peeks it's little head up from under the sofa cushions or pops out from behind your daughter's jacket on the back of a chair. Devil Child . . .

If you are like many people, you probably have a name for your remote. Whereas common names for humans might be Mary or John (or these days, more like Joshua and Katelyn, Caitlyn, Catelynn, or Kaitlyn), the most common remote control name seems to be "Thedamnthing"—as in, "Has anyone seen Thedamnthing?" Or "Darn it, where is Thedamnthing? Others give it a less personalized name—like the clicker, the flicker, or simply, the remote. It doesn't seem to matter what it's called, though—it doesn't listen to you anyhow.

Now remote controls have come a long way these days, in order to cover the wealth of audio and video technology available. Put together a wide screen high definition TV, a DVD player, a cassette deck, a five-speaker surround sound system, and you've either set yourself up for one expensive $400 universal remote or a TV tray full of individual remote controls. And as long as you've numbered the eight remotes you need to run all this stuff, you're fine.

But just turn your head, my friend, and those little buggers too are hopping off the tray, hiding under the couch, in the dog food bowl, or your underwear drawer. Because it's in their nature to roam. Perhaps that's why we call them "remotes."

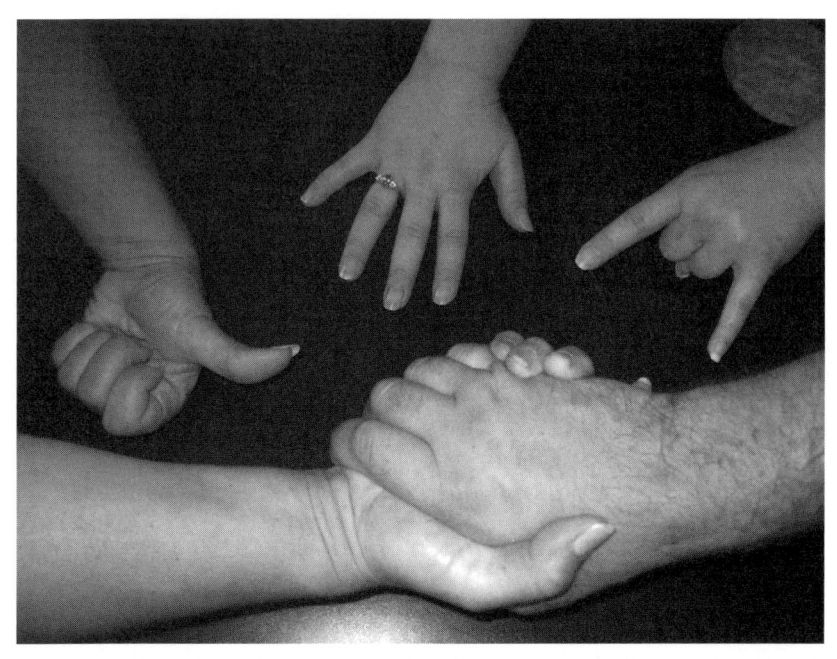

Carolyn, Deb, and Jim demonstrate a few of the many ways that people talk with their hands. Luckily, they didn't display that most popular of hand signals often flashed in high traffic situations and during domestic disputes . . . (Photo by Joe Paradis).

Two Cents, 7-21-05

Talking With the Hands

It's somewhat of an urban legend that certain ethnic peoples, in particular the Italians and French, just naturally use hand gestures to emphasize the points they are making as they speak. Having grown up in a French household and with an Italian wife, it is something I'm used to, something I do frequently myself, and something I think is a riot.

Her lips didn't move at all, but I knew what she was saying from across the parking lot. Her arms had shot up in a sweeping gesture and the hands were making continuous circular motions in the air. That meant, "I found the car. It's over here."

Most people around her stared somewhat questionably at all this arm flapping. But one little old lady nodded and smiled at her. "I am happy for you," she said, with just the hint of an Italian accent.

Such is the secret world of "talking with your hands," a mysterious form of communication to the majority of Americans who can calmly elicit a sentence without the need to move their arms from their sides or put down their coffee to draw imaginary pictures in the air. Some say it's a personal thing—that talking with the hands is simply a form of expression, which some individuals utilize to emphasize a point as they speak. But I'm here to say it's more than that. It's a natural motion and spiritual passion for certain nationalities.

Those with insomnia or extremely boring lives may notice the feeble attempts by politicians on C-SPAN to speak with their hands. Dozens of politicians strut to the podium daily in both the U.S. House of Representatives and the Senate to blab about things they think you might care about. Their speeches are often punctuated by arm-flailing and hand-ringing of the sort that might be misconstrued as talking with the hands. Indeed, a conversation with our own Congressman Jeb Bradley can lead one to step back a few paces, as his conversations are always accompanied by hand motions that mimic the tomahawk chop made famous by Atlanta Braves fans.

But political hand-ringing is far from talking with the hands. Most scholars who study the art seem to concede that politicians are certainly not talking with their hands—they're simply flailing about. Such politicking is an art in itself.

Real talking with the hands is much more than that. It's half a dozen elderly gentlemen sitting on a park bench, talking across one another's conversations. Looking like one of those Motown singing groups, with the arms and legs moving in unison with their words.

Talking with the hands is two teenage girls sitting on the front steps, chattering excitedly about boyfriends, as their hands punctuate the air around them.

It's a group of guys gathered around the big screen TV watching a Red Sox game. Mimicking the 'safe' sign flashed by an umpire as Johnny Damon steals second base. And arguing playfully with one another over every call, chin to chin, arms pumping up and down like a Richard Simmons "Sweating to the Oldies" workout.

To me, talking with the hands is best exemplified by the large holiday gatherings we used to spend around my in-laws' dinner table. Eighteen or so of us, most of them Italian. Passing the food, passing the conversation. People having a good time. Arms going this way and that as the words became more pronounced, with hand motions that increased in speed accordingly. Wine being spilled. Meatballs flying. An occasional wedding ring sailing across the table and landing in the calamari.

Many Italians proudly claim to be the originators of talking with the hands. From my experience, they certainly do a lot of it. Witness St. Peter's Square at the Vatican any year, as the Pope celebrates Easter Sunday Mass. It's 100,000 Italians who appear to be doing The Wave at Fenway Park. Some of them could slice romano cheese paper-thin with a wave of the open palms and a little emphasis. Or whip up waves on a calm pond with that constant rotation of the forearms, reminiscent of the blades on an old-fashioned push lawnmower.

But I'm not sure I'm ready to concede top dog status to Italians as the only nationality that can expertly talk with the hands. As a Frenchman (God help me), I seem to do a fair amount of it myself. And my wife understands my own hand motions as I signal back to her from across the parking lot. I'm fairly proud of knowing a "second language."

So the next time you find yourself around the water cooler at work, discussing last night's American Idol winners, put down the coffee cup and add a few swings of the hand to emphasize your verbal points. It's a catchy habit. Just don't break the water cooler.

I wonder if these folks have dug the proper holes for lying in the sand? Comfort is key at the beach. (Photo by Joe Paradis).

Two Cents, 7-21-05

The Beach Date

When I tell you my wife is a saint, I really mean it. She has been the inspiration for a number of my story ideas—mostly because she is closest to me and I observe her actions more frequently than I do others. So naturally I write about them. I've received more positive comments about this story than any other—and Joanne received a huge, spontaneous vote of good-natured sympathy from many readers, for "allowing me" to write about personal moments. But don't tell me you haven't experienced similar beach episodes in your life—we saw you a few blankets over from us, basking in the sun. And I wrote it all down . . .

"How about the beach?" I asked.

"The beach?"

"Yeah, let's go to the beach. It'll be our date for this month." I had to try hard with this one. Joanne isn't really that keen about going to the beach. All that sand that gets lodged between her toes. The bathing suit wedgies. Seaweed and cigarette butts that dot the shoreline. She's not generally a big fan of the beach.

So I talked fast. "We'll go early, take the Miata, cruise up the coastline, stop for lunch. It'll be fun. Our first time at the beach without kids in 16 years . . . "

I held that last sentence in mid air, playing, I suppose, the sympathy card.

"Okay," was her simple response. I nearly fell over. The kids were chortling in the background. "MOM's going to the beach?" guffawed my daughter. They were bent over laughing. Rolling on the rug, clutching their sides. We're always pleased that we can keep our kids so entertained.

We woke early that next morning, one of those hot sticky Saturdays we've been experiencing all summer. And I knew this might be tough. Past excursions to the beach, kids in tow, have been the primary reason we always had an SUV. A vehicle that could support the weight of all the stuff we brought with us.

So I didn't say anything when I saw a few dozen items forming a pile on the dining room table. Several kinds of sun block. Apples, granola bars, grapes, sunglasses, paperback books, towels, flip flops. Bottles of water. The Miata's trunk holds the equivalent of a duffel bag. I was beginning to worry. But lo and behold, it all fit into a small cooler and a beach bag. And we were off by 9 a.m., cruising up Route 101 toward Hampton.

It was a nice day and we took it slowly. Kept the top up to avoid that hair flail that women riding in convertibles hate. We caught up with a line of other little two-seater convertibles, apparently all heading for the coast. Not one of the passengers was under forty years of age. We felt comfortable. In the groove. Older than dirt.

We made it to Hampton in forty minutes, and headed for the parking lot at the far end of the beach. We experienced our first use of a 4-hour parking token. Beats stuffing quarters in the meter every hour. Had to stop a park ranger to ask about those. He pleaded with us to go to the ranger office at the other end of the beach to purchase our token for five dollars. He really didn't want us to spend an extra buck to purchase the same token at the sub shop across the street. His concern was touching and I thanked him as he wrote up a $25 ticket for the car next to us whose meter had run out. I ran over to the sub shop as Joanne stood by the car.

We grabbed our stuff from the trunk and literally ran across the sand, it was that hot. We settled in next to an elderly couple, who were just breaking out their lunch. It was 10 a.m. The gentleman was seated in his beach chair, while his wife was just rolling over on to her knees in a valiant attempt to get up from the blanket. She had half a sandwich hanging out of her mouth, bologna and cheese slices flapping in the wind. Thank God I wasn't hungry, because I lost my appetite right there.

We were struck by the quiet around us—except for the grunting of that woman rolling around the blanket, as her husband stared off into the waves, thoughtfully chewing his hamburger. It struck me that there were no teens on the beach. None. But then I realized that they don't rise until noon when they can sleep in.

We laid out the blanket and my wife began smoothing out the lumps under it. Good housekeeping, that girl. Then she started making two little indentations in the sand and I watched with curiosity as she settled chest down on the blanket, filling those two holes with that part of her body—if you catch my drift. I have never ever seen this before. Struck me as something that exotic animals might do in the pages of National Geographic, before laying their eggs.

She had already smeared herself with SPF 30 sunblock. You could walk on the sun with that strengh of sunblock and not burn. She then laid out the plan—half an hour on her stomach, then half an hour on her back. It would be an equalized tan, something the 400-lb gentleman a few blankets down could have heeded. He had some tremendous blotches across his back, alternating bright red and pasty white where he had tried to slap the sun block on. There's one guy who was bound to have a restless sleep tonight . . .

I lied down next to the wife and discovered how difficult it is to chew gum when your cheek is resting on the sand. So I rolled on my side, catching the sounds of several languages in the air. With my eyes closed, I imagined I was lounging at the U.N. swimming pool or a Saddam Hussein sympathy rally. Together, we eavesdropped on a loud family of large people, grazing a few yards from us. The loudmouth mother was regaling her sister with tales of her and her husband's travels throughout the world. Like no one else travels. I silently prayed for her to develop laryngitis—for the sake of all of us within a mile of her.

We did get down to the water and even into it. I bobbed up and down for a few moments near a Cambodian gentleman who kept smiling at me. I always wonder about people who do that. So I inched away till he started smiling at someone else. Must be a happy guy.

But Joanne and I had a good time on our beach date. Five hours of sun, our first tans all year. We walked the shoreline and enjoyed the day and the relaxation we're hardly ever able to find in those busy lives we all lead.

We rode back home with the top down. Who really cared at that point? It's great to be alive.

The first day of college is a bit different for those who enter the Reserve Officer Training Corps program (ROTC). Especially when your first "teacher" at Indoctrination is a Marine Corps Gunnery Sergeant and Drill Instructor of 20 years (left), who stands out just a tad from the more relaxed Navy instructors next to him. (Photo by Joe Paradis).

Two Cents, 9-01-05

A Taste of College, Maine Style

As a parent, I think one of the most difficult times in life is when you finally let your children go out into the real world on their own. Now I'm talking about teenage children here—not the ones who are my age and have recycled back to your house because their marriage broke up or they can't pay their rent. But watching teenagers leave the roost -whether to start college, join the military, work, or just bum around Europe for a year—that's an emotional time for a parent. Such was the case when we sent our first child, Robert, off to the wilds of northern New England and the University of Maine in the fall of 2005.

Those of us sending the kiddies off to college this week are feeling a tremendous, albeit bittersweet weight lifted from our shoulders. Finally, we'll be able to see the top of the dining room table again, as boxes of school supplies, bags of clothing, sheets, towels, pillows, and piles of non-perishable foods can soon be carted out to the truck. Finally, the front hall can be cleared of the new microwave oven, the mini-refrigerator, the 28" television, the laptop, the printer, and the mountain bike. Somewhere in that pile, I hope there might also be a book or two, although I saw none in our pile. Maybe they get those at school. Hopefully they get those at school . . .

Yep, it'll be nice to use the table for its intended purpose again. And to come through the front door without crawling over a mountain of boxes.

Our family had a little prelude this year, before sending our oldest cherub off to college. His presence was respectfully requested by the U.S. Navy for four days of fun in the sun at Maine Maritime Academy before beginning classes at the University of Maine under a ROTC scholarship. Upon graduation, he'll then spend four years playin' in the mud as a Marine Corps officer, something he proudly wants to do—which makes us proud as well.

We drove up on Tuesday night, a blissful six-hour drive among the trees, the travelers, and the Mainiacs, stopping for a night at a small town hotel, with small town beds and a smaller town bathroom. The next morning, we drove another hour out to Maine Maritime. We passed at least fifty yard sales on the way. Now there aren't a hundred houses in the area, so they either buy each other's crap or wait for the unsuspecting, like us, to drive by. They were all out there at 7:00 a.m., prepping for business. Fantastic Barn Sale touted one sign. I didn't see a barn anywhere. We were relieved to escape into the Academy, where parents got to meet the ROTC staff. The kids got to fill out government paperwork, always an experience, and shake in their boots, anticipating "things yet to come" that day.

We met a happy little guy named Lieutenant Joy, the Navy instructor. Also met a more serious guy named Captain Grim, who is the Marine officer assigned to the unit. Joy and Grim ... could there ever be a better mix of what these kids are in for?

We all met in an auditorium with Navy Captain Kopang, who is in command of the unit. He explained the ROTC program, an excellent one by all standards. He also informed the kids that they should eat a "light lunch," as they would be meeting Gunnery Sergeant Merrill that afternoon. "If there's one thing you will never forget about this program," he intoned deadpan, "it will be Gunnery Sergeant Merrill." I glanced down the row at the kids I was near. Sweat was beading off of their foreheads. Hands were wrung. Lunch was a somber, reflective time. Parents left shortly thereafter.

For the next four days, under the watchful eye of Gunnery Sergeant Merrill, a true Marine Corps drill instructor, my son and nineteen other ROTC students were "invited" to endured just a taste of that little bit of hell we call Basic Training. Good preparation for any college kid. Maybe it should be a required course.

We drove back up on Saturday to pick up our "hardened Marine." The ROTC staff held a little ceremony, swore them all in, and presented each with his Navy or Marine pin. The kids looked sharp. We had a typical military picnic afterwards to celebrate. They rolled out the gas grill, lined up two tables in this huge gymnasium, and we chowed down.

Before leaving, we stopped in the bookstore for a few things, and heard our boy saying "Yes, Ma'am" and "Aye, Sir" to everyone he met. I told him that I expected to be addressed as Sir from now on. I don't think that will happen. We were on the road an hour later.

On the way home, we decide to celebrate. Stopped at a roadside stand to buy a pie and some corn from Priscilla and Stanley Metcalf, pie crust entrepreneurs, who shared a few teeth between them. Priscilla was definitely in charge, directing the operation from her lawn chair. With only eight ears of corn on the table, I asked for a dozen. "Well, you count those up there . . ." she said.

"Yes, ma'am," I found myself saying.

". . . and you take four more out of that box over there. Five dollars please." I'm sure she'll put out another eight ears when we leave.

My wife asked Stanley how much the pies were.

"Sixteen dollars," he smiled, showing off his tooth. I know she was about to walk away, but I said we'd take one. Priscilla also reminded us to call and special order our next pie. Gave us her business card. I told her next time we wanted to drive six hours for a pie, we'd be sure to drop by. She flashed her tooth. We ran to the car. I love Maine.

We arrived home in the dark and stumbled through that mountain of school stuff still in the front hall. It will all be gone next week, I told myself—along with our son. But somehow, having just experienced a glimpse of his future and realizing we soon wouldn't be seeing his smiling face around every day, I wasn't quite as anxious to clear the table of all his stuff. I patted him on the back, as we walked through the door, and he turned and smiled. This "growing up" phase sure is hard on parents.

There's so much to see at the dump (oops . . . the Recycle Center) that one picture just doesn't do it justice. But I tried. (Photo by Joe Paradis).

Two Cents, LT and NN, 9-22-05

Dump Guys

This story apparently so moved the gentleman who manages the Saturday recycle center in town, that he wrote me a thank you letter. I was touched. In "the old days," a trip to the town dump was a Saturday ritual. It's where you met the neighbors, where your kids ran around on mounds of steaming trash, looking for anything cool to take home. Today, that has changed in many communities, for the better obviously. Now we have recycling centers, where we drop off construction materials, metal, old computers, all for a fee to dispose of them. Everything's now cleaner, compartmentalized, more efficient in the trash business. But the interesting characters still come out, just as in the old days. I'm one of them. And here's my story.

It was an early start for sure. But for these quality outings, it's always worth it. On this beautiful Saturday morning, I spent an hour piling everything in the back of the truck—careful not to scratch the paint—stopped off at Dunkin' Donuts for a coffee, and headed off down the road with a song in my heart. Yes, I was on my way to . . . the dump.

Now okay, it's technically not the dump in our town. It's the Drop Off Center. And we can't just dump stuff there in a big pile as in days of yore. We now back our vehicles up a steep hill to the edge of a dumpster and drop our junk off the side—hence the name Drop Off Center, I guess. There are separate dumpsters for metal and others for construction materials, which include everything else that isn't specifically collected. They gather TVs, batteries, and tires in separate containers. All very neat and clean. Yes, sir, a nice, clean dump.

This beautiful morning, I was greeted by a smiling attendant at the hallowed gates of the drop off center. As polite as a waiter in any first-class restaurant, he looked over my load, pretending to take my word for what was buried in there. But he really didn't. I caught his sideward glance behind our old grill, the little peak he stole under the pile of rotten wood. I was dealing with a real professional here—he knew all the tricks that a dishonest dumper might try to pull. He gave me a price.

I gave him a check. Paying to drop off your trash—a concept as strange as paying to watch TV for those who grew up with three free channels and the town dump right around the corner.

I stepped out of the truck, just to stretch a bit before ascending the slope. I breathed in deeply, expecting to capture a taste of that vibrant dump air that I recalled from my youth. But of course, it wasn't the same. The smell of old wood, plasterboard, and rusted metal, all neatly contained in huge dumpsters, just doesn't come close to those steaming piles of dump junk, containing God-knows-what hazardous materials, garbage, and tires from my early years. But I stretched anyhow. It just seemed the respectable thing to do.

Three other vehicles were at the edge of the construction materials dumpster when I backed my truck up. Two gentlemen and a lady. One of the guys hiked his pants over a huge belly and, with a nod and tip of the hat, acknowledged my presence. The other bellowed out a hearty "Good morning!" as if we were a couple of pals in the neighborhood gym before a squash game—although this guy looked like he grew squash rather than played squash. The suspenders and John Deere cap gave him away. Just two regular guys. Dump guys. My kinda guys.

The woman was of a different caliber. Dressed as if for a casual walk around the block, she completely ignored us, intent on clearing her trunk of its neatly stacked piles of wood. Now, a true dump guy would have burned that wood in his fireplace or wood stove, or maybe begun to build a shed or fishing boat with it. But I have to credit the woman for bringing her pile o' wood to the dump rather than hiding it in her curbside trash bags. And I was smitten with her colorful lime green garden gloves . . . another reason why we have a clean dump. But I'll bet she still stopped off at McDonald's rest room on the way home, just to wash her hands. A dump is, after all, only so clean.

I was glad to have arrived early, beating the crowd to this popular weekend retreat. Well fortified with nutritious coffee and a low fat, cholesterol-free coconut donut (not), I had the energy to heave the remains of my dilapidated shed and an old couch into the belly of that dumpster, enjoying every crunching sound. Like any guy, I relish the opportunity to smash things in a safe environment—that is, away from my wife's watchful eye. No doubt, a throwback to caveman days. My dump buddies enjoyed it too. They had already tossed their loads in and were just leaning against their trucks, standing in pools of sweat and learning to breath again. But they still had enough stamina to goad me on with every toss of my stuff. I felt like Superman.

Alas, the joy ended all too soon. The bed of my truck emptied quickly. I swept it out, descended from the slope, and stepped out of the cab for one more quick sniff before leaving. It's not the same, but I'll just have to get used to this new, cleaner dump smell—excuse me, this Drop Off Center smell. Then I headed home for a shower. Some smells you do have to wash away.

It was a tough night of Trivial Pursuit for Brian that New Year's Eve. Luckily for him, we were all in a tolerant mood that night . . . after a few hours of ribbing him incessantly for his prowess on the game board. (Photo by Joe Paradis).

Two Cents, 1-12-06

A New Year's That Might Have Been

Few people can recall their first New Year's Eve celebration. It was either so long ago that they forgot it. Or they were a bit under the influence and couldn't even remember the very next day, whether or not they had a good time. And as the years pass, New Year's Eve just becomes another day, where you might stay awake right up till midnight—or you might not. It's no big deal either way. But it's always good to spend it with friends, have a few laughs, and enjoy each other's company. Even if you do forget what you did by the time the next New Year's Eve rolls around . . .

Had you spent the New Year's weekend in a roomy old inn in Jackson NH, you might have wished the torrential downpours were snow instead of rain. It would have, after all, saved you an hour's ride through Franconia Notch up to Breton Woods, where the new snow measured eight inches and the old temperature eight degrees. Had you not chickened out, you might have spent a few hours on the slopes bonding with your kids in that chilled-to-the-bone weather, instead of smiling at them from the warmth of the lodge each time one or another of them flopped down the mountain on some part of their bodies.

While at Breton Woods, you might have roamed the regal halls of the Mount Washington Hotel like a professional Japanese tourist, clicking off picture after picture of one of New Hampshire's truly majestic turn-of-the-century hotels. You might have pretended to be a tour guide, as you escorted friends on a mock tour of the hotel's many hallways, pointing out features and people, and concocting stories on the spot that others might have taken for gospel as they listened in on your diatribe.

That night, you might have eaten dinner in the cozy dining hall of your inn, and perhaps smiled at the gentleman who actually skipped through the dining room to his table, with four or five children trailing behind. You might have later named him Skippy and cursed him silently, as those wonderful little cherubs spent the next hour skipping up and down, up and down, up and down the aisle. Perhaps, rather than trip them on their next pass by your table, you might have wisely instructed your friend to notify the maitre d' of the stress this was causing other diners. Perhaps she in turn, might have notified Skippy of the inclination of others who, while they all generally love children, would not mind throwing his uncaring body through the inn's beautiful plate glass window into the snow.

You might have loved eating out each night that weekend, but perhaps become just a wee bit tired of the soup selections everywhere you ate. While always delicious, a steady diet of either clam chowder or French onion soup might have conjured up thoughts of Russian peasants and the staple of cabbage soup that they consume daily throughout their long, hard winter months.

You might have spent hours playing card games and board games with your friends that weekend. And enjoyed the awkwardness of bringing the coffee table from your room down to your friends' room, in order to make a larger playing surface. You might have enjoyed the questioning looks on the faces of other patrons, as they spotted you coming down the hall with your table. And you might have told them not to worry—you'd be in their room next to inspect for illegal coffee tables.

You might have cracked up during a fierce game of "Trivial Pursuit, The '90s," when your friend could not get the correct answer "Jamaica," even when given a hint that the answer began with a "J" and ended with "amaica." Or when another of his answers was "George Clooney," and the hints you gave him included "Rosemary's nephew" and "George C. Looney"; yet he still came back with a blank stare. It might have been a night to make fun of exhausted people—and you might certainly have made the best of it.

You might have enjoyed shopping the outlets for an entire day, something you have never done. Searching out those after-Christmas bargains to the point where your wife and daughter, professional shoppers in their own right, might have become physically exhausted. Yet, after a brief sojourn by your party into Brookstone to play with the massage chairs, you might have continued to root out brand name pants, shirts, and jackets for less than $10 each, including one pair of cranberry—not red—corduroys.

Perhaps you might have topped off your New Year's Eve at a gala event, featuring some of the oldest jazz musicians in the Valley. Wishing fervently for a rousing jazz flute solo, a la the movie "Anchorman," that never came. But, alas, it was not to be and you may have retired to your chambers early enough to witness the pain of Dick Clark hosting the countdown to 2006 in Times Square.

Or maybe you didn't experience any of those things this past New Year's weekend. But some dummy did—and he might have decided to write about them. Perhaps.

The Pause... Honoring Three Young Men

Well here you are, half way through this book of short stories. Good for you! Hopefully, you were able to sit back on the couch, hunker down in your favorite chair, or find a few moments on the toilet to grab a quick story, among other things (don't worry, I'm not offended). And I hope you've been able to find something that made you smile, chuckle, or even outright laugh. Perhaps even elicit a hearty guffaw or two from that mouth of yours. I would hope so anyhow. Humor is good for the soul.

But, as we both know, life is not all fun and games. That's why I'd like to pause in this section of the book, to bring you three stories I wrote about three different young men who left this world many years before they should have. They were all friends and schoolmates of my son, and their passing—all in the span of a few years—left a mark on the town of Londonderry, particularly among its young people. A mark that will hopefully live with them throughout their lives, as they never forget their friends.

These are not strictly stories of tragedy, although the circumstances under which each of these boys died certainly were tragic. These are, instead, stories that celebrate their lives, the kind of kids they were, and the joy which they brought to their parents and all of us who knew them. It is within the encouragement they gave to us, that we find the strength to truly appreciate that "it's great to be alive."

Unfortunately, it's not difficult, these days, to find many kids who have met similar fates. Kids who will never had the chance to reach adulthood, to raise their own families, to enjoy grandchildren. Surely, we all know some of them. Because they died young, they are frozen in time—always to be remembered for their vibrant youth, maybe their innocence, perhaps their lust for life. And for those who believe, we know they are safe in Heaven, because our time on earth is just a testing ground for something far greater.

So pause here for a moment and read about PJ, Justin, and Herbert. Celebrate their lives with me, and reflect a bit. Then, we'll return to a few more chuckles and guffaws. I don't think these three young men would have wanted it any other way.

A picture worth a thousand words! Lance Corporal PJ Sora, USMC, photographed in 2003, with Erika Harold, Miss America (left) and Candice Glickman, Miss New Hampshire. What young guy wouldn't have a smile on his face? PJ's mother, Gail, wasn't sure whether we should use this picture at first, but what better way to remember a young man than in his finest moments? She happily agreed. At the reception following PJ's burial service at the NH Veterans Cemetery, I watched Gail bravely encourage PJ's friends, who were preparing to become Marines, to be the best that they could be. PJ was probably smiling over that too . . . (Photo courtesy of Peter and Gail Sora).

Two Cents, LT, 05-20-04
Why We Have Heroes

PJ Sora is an American hero. He became one of my son's best friends from their time together as fellow trumpeters with the Londonderry Lancers, our high school marching band. PJ had always wanted to be a Marine, that interesting kind of warrior who runs toward the guns in battle, rather than away from them. And he became one. Tragically, he died while on training maneuvers, prior to being shipped to Iraq. This is the story of how I watched my son absorb the news of his friend's death and learned to deal with it. A tall order for a 16-year old. A taller order for a young Marine's family.

Brave servicemen and women like PJ willingly become sacrifices for our American way of life. Brave people like their parents endure the loss of a child quietly and stoically, so that you and I can enjoy that way of life. Remember PJ Sora and his fellow brothers and sisters who have fallen. Remember why you have the freedoms that you do.

He just lay on his bed, staring at the ceiling. He stayed that way for several hours, until finally crawling under the covers for a fitful night's sleep. His afternoon had been spent in solidarity with his friends, consoling one another, probably more with their collective presence than any number of words. I'll never really know though. This wasn't a world into which I was invited.

My son and his friends had just heard of the untimely death of their friend, PJ Sora. A corporal in the Marine Corps, 19-year old PJ had been killed in a HUMVEE accident while on training maneuvers in California. His next destination was to have been Iraq.

PJ was one of my son's first friends when he joined the Lancers High School Marching Band three years ago. PJ was a senior. Robert was a freshman. They met at Andy Soucy's annual Band Camp, a unique environment that makes it easy for freshmen and seniors to actually become friends, free from the stigma of high school hierarchy that usually makes that improbable. The bond was instantaneous. Our rather shy son had met someone he could admire.

Robert was only once disappointed by PJ. That was during his first week of high school, when PJ treated him like the freshman he was—the same initiation everyone goes through during that first week when they finally get to high school. Bumping him in the hallway. Kicking the back of his chair in class. But after that, the two trumpet players got along quite well—and were probably the stronger for it.

PJ was a compact kid. He had a ready smile and a sense of humor that made you like him. He had confidence too. And he seemed to know what he really wanted to do with his life, even before others did. PJ wanted to be a Marine.

But my intimate knowledge of PJ ends there. I know that he had enlisted in the Marine Corps Reserves after trying college for a year. He later signed up for active duty. You would see him all over town, dressed in his 'blues', displaying that uniform, of which he was so proud. He was always speaking to his friends about the Maine Corps and trying to talk them into seeing the recruiter. The Corps often uses its own to recruit others. Camaraderie builds solidarity. Solidarity builds the Corps.

PJ's parents have a flagpole in their front yard. It displays the American flag and, of course, the Marine Corps flag. PJ made sure of that. Those flags fly at half mast these days. His room was covered with Marine Corps paraphernalia too, according to Robert's last visit there. He was particularly awed by a large knife PJ had. One that he told Robert he used to shave the hair on his arms. PJ was a Marine through and through.

So why is it that a kid with such a bright future had to leave us so soon? Why is it that PJ's wonderful parents are forced to bury their child, an event that no parent should ever have to experience? There are no answers that could fully satisfy the heaviness they must feel in their hearts. Only those who have experienced a similar loss can ever really identify with them.

The rest of us look at them from afar, as I did at PJ's wake and his funeral. Profoundly awed by the strength which his family displayed in the face of this soul-searing tragedy. Proud of what a kid like PJ had accomplished, but knowing, all too well, that he will physically accomplish no more on this earth.

As I stood quietly at the funeral at St. Jude Church last week, I tried to reconcile why my son was lying on his bed, staring up at the ceiling for hours. Maybe he was looking to PJ in heaven. And maybe PJ was looking down. Ready to kick the back of Robert's chair once again. That's the way PJ would do things to get you going.

Semper Fi, PJ. You got us all going.

Justin Young was a trumpeter in the Lancers Marching Band from Londonderry High School, when he died in July 2004, just before his senior year. His bandmates resolved to leave his trumpet untouched in his storage bin for that next year, as a tribute to Justin. (Photo courtesy of Steve Young).

Two Cents, 7-15-04

Remembering Justin

Justin Young was the epitome of the average teenage boy. He had that mix of curiosity and mischievousness, with an occasional spate of quietness and reflection, that parents just know will, in the end, mold a boy into a solid contributor to society. But Justin, alas, was destined to remain that fun-loving teen in the memories of those who knew him. In July of 2004, Justin lost his life in a small airplane accident, when flying back home with his dad from a weekend camping trip. His dad survived the crash and fought valiantly to regain his own life and health. He lives today with memories of that day . . . often speaking publicly of the serenity he discovered as he laid pinned inside that cockpit, knowing that his son, sitting right next to him, had already committed his soul up to God. Only those who lose a child can really understand that. The rest of us can only marvel at his ability to carry on . . . and remember our friend Justin as he was. This is my tribute to Justin Young.

New York City's St. Patrick's Day Parade, March 2004. I entered the hotel room to inform the boys that they had five minutes to be dressed and down for breakfast. Suddenly, two more kids popped up from under a pile of blankets on the floor and ran down to their own rooms to get dressed. Justin was one of them.

Rose Bowl Parade, January 2004. A bit of "boys will be boys" antics in the hotel parking lot led to one kid being taken to the hospital for a bit of a cut. Yep, that was Justin.

Medieval Times Restaurant & Show, Pasadena CA, January 2004. A group of band kids dressed in their traditional tin foil armor while waiting for dinner. They call themselves the "Knights of the Oblong Table." Oh yeah, Justin was among them.

A quiet kid rushed into his Dad's business after school and headed right for the computer, either for the video games or perhaps a bit of homework. Who really knows. But you know—that was Justin.

He could walk into a room full of strangers and win an award for the quietest kid in the world. He could walk into a room full of kids he knew and just start cracking them up. He was funny. Goofy funny, some kids would say. A charming kid. A really good friend.

But he's gone now. And that's the painful reality of it. Accidents happen, and a friend of mine sits in a hospital this week, battered, bruised and just out of critical danger himself, questioning his decisions and his abilities. Asking himself why, in the throws of an airplane mishap, his son died . . . and he did not. I can't even begin to comprehend that kind of pain. And I can only feel helpless, not knowing how to properly help him, without seeming to pry into his family's private life.

Justin Young was a good kid. We tend to say that about every kid who meets tragedy, don't we? But this kid—he was a good kid. Really. And as they did during the loss of another friend, PJ, several months ago, a remarkable group of Justin's friends, band kids mostly, put their "contacts machine" in motion last week and gathered together, on a moment's notice, to honor this funny kid. To console one another. To ask all the usual questions for which there are no real answers. To salve a wound that will take a long, long time, if ever, to heal.

But those with faith, real faith, know that Justin is in a good place now. We weep for our loss and the loss of his family. But we know he's where we can only hope to be some day. And there is peaceful comfort in that.

But as we ache from that loss, let us not forget his family, for they really need our prayers and our support. A good man, who has done so much to unselfishly help our community, has lost his son. And he needs us to help him pull through. Because the best traits of a lost son linger in the soul of his father. And we need to help him find them again.

Two Cents, 01-10-07

A Tribute to Herbert

Herbert Darling was a high school classmate of my son. The Class of 2005, Londonderry, New Hampshire. A truly gifted and affable kid, Herbert was respected by his peers and adults alike. And as the Class of '05 headed off to different colleges, many kept in touch, primarily through Facebook or MySpace or some other internet technology. Occasionally they'd get together. Herbert attended one of those gatherings a few days before Christmas last year. And tragically, fell to his death from a second floor balcony. The world truly lost an exceptional young man. I felt compelled to write about Herbert because so many knew him. And will miss him. And although we'll carry his memory in our hearts, his mother won't be able to kiss him goodbye again. His dad won't be able to hug him. And that is the ultimate hole that the loss of a child—especially an only child—sears into a parent's soul. This story is a tribute to a wonderful young man. Make sure you save a couple of seats for your folks in heaven, Herbert. Good boy.

It finally did hit me. As I shook the last hand in a long line of grieving relatives, my eyes began filling with tears and I had to clench my jaw and look to the sky, just to maintain some sort of composure. It's a guy thing, I know. But when you've just spent several excruciatingly long minutes, weeping and commiserating with friends who lost their only son two days before Christmas, your emotions are the only outlet for coping with the feeling of utter helplessness that engulfs your soul.

Herbert E. Darling III left this world on December 23, 2006, at the tender age of 19. The practical side of me asked the immediate question—how. How did this happen? What were the circumstances? But the spiritual side of me asked the more important question—why. Why did this happen? Why to Herbert, of all kids? A young man who had everything going for him. An Honors student and demonstrated leader to his peers. A kid who could laugh freely, who always had a kind word. Someone with that infectious enthusiasm for life that comes only with youth.

An impressive young man, Herbert Darling was respected by both adults and his peers, and had much to look forward to at Loyola University, with a bright future beyond. (Photo courtesy of Herb and Lucy Darling).

But I have no business asking how or why Herbert had to leave us. I have no right to question it at all. Life is as it is—a roller coaster ride of ups and downs, of good and bad. Filled with both happiness and sorrow, incredible highs and devastating lows. God gives each of us a slice of that life to work with and there is neither rhyme nor reason as to how long that life might be.

So I can only thank God for allowing us the pleasure of having known Herbert for a short time and been a small part of his life. I can only remember him as a friend of my son, as a kid roundly admired by both his peers and their parents. Respected by his teachers and teammates. Loved by his parents and friends.

And I will always carry my own fond memories of Herbert . . .

I will remember the skinny little kid who played Panther football, swimming in his oversized shoulder pads and constantly adjusting his glasses.

I will remember a high school Honors student sitting next to Mrs. Mee at endless School Board meetings. A natural student representative to the School Board. Always alert, always articulate, as he traveled quite comfortably in the presence of adults.

I will remember the young man who organized a charter bus ride, with forty or so of his closest friends, for their Senior Prom. I will always be thankful for Herbert's and his parents' hospitality in opening their house to those kids and their parents for refreshments and pictures before that huge, purple bus pulled up the driveway.

I will remember an excited kid in a flowing blue robe, hugging girl after girl at his high school graduation. Leaving jealous fathers in the crowd exchanging glances with one another and wondering why we couldn't have been like that when we graduated high school years ago.

My wife and I will remember those chance encounters with Herbert's mother in the aisles of Shaw's Supermarket, where we would proudly exchange stories about how well our boys were doing in colleges on opposite sides of the country. We hope those encounters still happen, because we all need to cross that bridge of awkwardness that this abrupt change in life has forced on Lucy and Herb.

And finally, I will always remember Herbert's little patch of chin hair, something that seems to sprout from every boy's chin once he reaches college. He certainly looked the epitome of a film school student, didn't he?

I will also never forget the tribute to this fine young man who was waked on December 28, 2006 . . .

I will never forget an all-too-soon reunion of Londonderry High School's Class of 2005, gathering in sorrow that day, to say goodbye to their friend and classmate and comfort one another. A Class that has not quite reached adulthood, yet has already experienced their share of friends taken too early in life.

I will never forget Herbert's fraternity brothers, in solidarity at his wake, who traveled from around the country to honor Herbert and his family. Guys who sat silently along the wall at the funeral home, each with a single white rose in his lapel, somber testimony to a brother who will always live in their hearts.

I will remember most vividly, Herbert's parents, standing humbly among so many friends and family members, and yet so all alone in the depths of their sorrow. A sorrow that, I am certain, only those who have experienced the loss of a child can truly understand.

So that night, as I stood with my family outside Peabody Funeral Home and gazed upon the hundreds of friends stretching in a line to the end of the driveway, waiting patiently to pay their respects, I couldn't help but think that God must have a plan for Herbert. He has to. And I pray that Herbert's parents may take comfort from that probability—and feel Herbert's steady hand on their shoulders as he guides them through a life that he will always live.

It doesn't have automatic windows and door locks, but it does have air conditioning, four tires, and an automatic starter. And that puddle dripping underneath the car is snow, not leaking oil. So, our daughter, Danielle, wasn't too unhappy to finally back her "new" Ford Focus, with 98,000 miles on it, down the driveway, after passing her driver's test—while I hid in the basement and crossed my fingers. (Photo by Joe Paradis).

Two Cents, 4-20-06

First Freedom

Parents are a funny breed. We spend a couple of years teaching our kids to walk, talk and poop in the toilet. Most of them get all that right. Then we spend another dozen years teaching them the importance of manners, education, good grooming, fair play, and hard work. Some of them get a few of those too. By the time they're teenagers, they think they've learned everything—and we're just about ready to let them go prove it to themselves. But there are a few hints along the way that turning them loose is tougher than we thought. One of those hints for me was when my daughter first got her driver's license. Read on . . .

She felt free at last. Able to take off when she wished (well . . . when they let her). To zip down the road, with no one looking over her shoulder. Without her father holding a ready hand on the emergency break. Or her mother reflexively clutching the door handle. She had joined the ranks of those who, on a daily basis, arm themselves with a ton of metal on wheels, with which they ply the roadways of America—and try to avoid tapping one another.

She was now a licensed driver. Watch out world.

From all accounts, it was a pretty easy journey. She contributed her savings toward her first car last fall and it sat in the driveway through most of the winter. She began learning driving techniques in earnest in March—always a barrel of fun for the teaching parents. The hallowed halls of drivers education class was her next step, with its parallel driving lessons from a professional driver. That's where she would unlearn the tried and true techniques her parents taught her, in favor of the new driving techniques. Like the new math, the new driving wouldn't make sense to her parents, or their parents, or their parents' parents. But if it kept her safe and cautious and law-abiding, that was just fine by her family.

Not of a generation that wastes a lot of time, she and nearly everyone in her drivers ed class traipsed down to the DMV the day after their final driving lessons. She admitted to being a bit nervous when she arrived there, although she really hadn't been nervous at all while practicing over the past few months. She drove herself all the way to Salem, her dad by her side, easing up his grip on the emergency brake just a bit. She took to the highway like a pro, chattering along for the entire 20-minute drive. Her attitude was just as it should be. A little loose, a little tight.

She zipped through the written test, proud to have gotten a better grade than her brother two years earlier—and didn't forget to tell him that when she called him later that day. She aced the driving test—a true credit to the DMV officer in Salem who administers that test. He's testimony to the type of officer who puts new drivers at ease, so that they can concentrate on their driving rather than worrying about a cop's stern demeanor.

Later that night, she bought her first tank of gas with twenty bucks her mom had given her. While her parents waited in their own car, she pumped the gas herself—just over nineteen dollars. She left the change at the gas station, not wanting to go back in to pick it up. Nothing like a tip for the oil companies. That won't happen again.

And when it was all over, and she had that shiny new driver's license in her hand, her dad hugged her warmly and proudly, his eyes closed tightly.

That hug unleashed a flood of thoughts for him. His little girl had just taken her first big step toward self-sufficiency. She was sixteen now, with the freedom to drive on her own. It wouldn't be long before she was off to college, probably away from home, probably in a big city somewhere. And he pictured her going on to graduate school or medical school and meeting some guy from Seattle—the bane of every father's existence—who might sweep his daughter away before her parents were really ready. She'd move to Indianapolis where she'd begin her career and never again camp with her parents in the White Mountains or body surf with them on Dawn Beach.

But those thoughts passed quickly and he smiled bravely. After all, this was her moment. And she'd have many more and he knew he'd be proud each time.

It's funny—the loss that freedom can bring . . .

Two Cents, 5-11-06

The Green, Green Grass of Home

I guess I'm what you'd call a lawn traditionalist. For years, I've always wanted to have "the perfect lawn." I once had it in my front yard, but that died many years ago for various reasons. I do want it again, but now I want less area to mow. So for several years I've been filling my sloping lawn area with tiered gardens. It's starting to work. But it's my backyard lawn that surprised me last year and it's of those sturdy grass seedlings that I write in this story.

For years, I've been struggling with the ultimate homeowner dilemma—growing a lawn of which I can be proud. Years ago, we had a front lawn to die for. A beautiful, dark green carpet of Kentucky bluegrass, rolling gracefully down our substantially sloped front lawn. A half acre of lovingly groomed grass that hungrily consumed every drop of water we were willing to feed it. And gobbled down bag after bag of lime and fertilizer. We could practically hear each blade of grass screaming for joy when the Chemlawn guy rolled up every other month. This was a lawn made for croquet, if it makes sense to play that sport on a slope.

I spent weeks preparing that lawn. I built my own sprinkler system. Hauled in six dump truckloads of loam (not "loom," as some people pronounce it), and spread the entire pile myself, by hand. I gave the tender seeds enough water to keep them growing, praying all along that the well wouldn't run dry. I talked to them encouragingly every night, as the evening mist touched their heads, and coaxed each of the young seedlings from its kernel. I raised those little sprouts. My babies. My green family.

But sadly, many families eventually go their own ways, and such was the case with my front lawn. A brutally hot summer, followed by a job "downsizing" that left my babies without their steady fix of Chemlawn fertilizer, ensured doom for our front lawn. The front yard slowly became a haven for crabgrass, and dandelions. We began to cultivate a pretty mean crop of milkweed each year. The once pristine carpet of bluegrass simply rolled itself up and disappeared.

Known simply as "Gnome with Fish" in our household, this little guy watches over the new lawn. I suspect he's been using the fish as fertilizer, because that grass has just taken off. (Photo by Joe Paradis).

My blind jealousy over losing my little green family, caused me to resent the once lovable little fellas. I resolved to do something about it . . . admittedly, after five years. I wanted as little grass as possible on that front lawn. I began tiering the slope, designing gardens and filling them with perennials. I built a brick walkway across the front of the house that ate up more of the front yard. I laid out an area for a granite and brick walkway and began a design for a patio, that I'll hopefully finish before the snow falls . . . maybe this year even.

But I also began a little covert operation . . . in the back yard. Three years ago, I secretly began seeding that lawn—thankfully, a much smaller patch of grass than the front. I was determined to prove to myself that I could really grow grass, that it wasn't just a fluke. That I hadn't lost my green thumb. I faithfully turned the sprinklers on it twice a day and fertilized with Scott's 4-in-1 formula. The results proved mediocre each fall, so I'd dump down more seed, following the instructions on the bag, and would start the cycle all over again the next spring. It had to kick in someday, I kept trying to convince myself. But other than a few additional patches here and there, it never did add much.

This year I resolved to try once again. But I decided to throw the instructions out. I trashed the 4-in-1 fertilizer formula and bought a giant bag of starter fertilizer. I roughed up the soil in all the bare spots, of which there were many, and poured down four times as much seed as recommended. And I set the sprinklers to provide a good soaking just once a day. Then I forgot about it. Went on to other projects—some electrical work, a bit of lattice construction, some pool preparation. Anything to keep me away from the backyard and that crazy checkerboard of green and brown squares. I couldn't bear it.

Then early one morning, about two weeks ago, I thought I heard faint screaming outside my bedroom window—like the desperate chirping of newly hatched chicks as they struggle to escape from their shells. Then the sprinklers came on. And the screams appeared to turn to giddy laughter; then to the kind of whooping you'd hear from a mariachi band. Still in a bit of a morning funk, I rolled out of bed, sleepy-eyed, and shuffled over to the window. And what to my wondering eyes should appear? A sea of grass, swaying back and forth like "The Wave" at a Red Sox game. Basking in a million droplets of water from the sprinkler, every blade of grass was squealing like a preschooler on the playground.

I couldn't believe my eyes. Before me lay the green meadow that Dorothy and her friends crossed on their way to Oz. That lush carpet of thick, rich grass, of which I've always dreamed.

Yep, my green family was back again. My babies. Sometimes, you just leave the kids alone and they grow up on their own. The only problem I see is that now I'll actually have to mow the lawn—at least in the backyard. The front slope, as always, is still a work-in-progress.

All agreed that my wife Joanne had the best hands for this photo. The rest of us have no fingernails. (Photo by Joe Paradis).

Two Cents, 5-25-06

Washing Your Hands —The Saving Grace

Except for the truly phobic, it's my impression that nobody really likes to wash their hands. I mean, we do it because we're supposed to, but it is, above all, an inconvenience. And you know how we hate to be inconvenienced. To have to traipse all the way across the kitchen floor to wash my hands before dinner . . . after all, I was just spreading manure in the garden. What's the big deal? Read on and find out— because it's better to wash your hands with soap, than to have your grandfather wash your mouth out with it . . .

Whenever my grandfather came to visit, it was always the first thing we had to do when my mother called us for dinner.

"Time to wash our hands, kids," he'd say. And like a gaggle of baby geese, the four of us would follow him into the bathroom, line up around the sink, and smear a little soap on our hands. Of course, as kids, we wiped more dirt on the towel than we washed down the drain. But the job was done and Grandpa was happy. He was a stickler for washing your hands before eating.

Other than those visits, I don't recall that we were ever forced to wash our hands before meals. That's probably because my mother pretty much had us wash our hands after everything we did. After a quick nose pick or those frequent trips to the bathroom. After playing outside or especially if we'd just touched money. "Do you know how many people have touched that money?" she'd ask. We couldn't fool Mom. Like her father, she too was a stickler.

Now this ingrained awareness of the need for clean hands has stayed with me throughout the years. I instinctively note those guys who sneak out of the men's room without washing. Generally, they glance around quickly to see if anyone's looking, and then walk very quickly toward the exit. Deep inside, they know that their mothers instructed them, years ago, to wash their hands after these private moments. They know they're breaking the rules of etiquette. But they also know their moms won't be coming into a men's room to check on them. So they test the limits. The shame of it all. Of course, as they sneak out of these public rest rooms, the 'unclean' also grab the doorknob with their soiled hands, which I'm sure has the line of guys at the sink wondering "How am I gonna get outta here ungermed?" But realistically, I've not seen anyone die from that. Not yet.

Now there are those guys who like to make sure everyone knows that they've washed their hands before exiting the men's room. They usually come out still wiping their wet hands on a paper towel, as if they're so busy that they just couldn't finish the job behind closed doors. Proof positive that they are as clean as God. It's an impressive ceremony, as they nonchalantly touch the towel in the nearest trashcan to cap this feat.

I once had a co-worker who said she would gauge the caliber of a person by the cleanliness of his or her hands. If she saw any dirt under the fingernails of a guy she was interviewing, she wouldn't even think about hiring him. Now, these guys would be doing manual labor, so a little dirt under the nails isn't inconceivable. But, nope, they wouldn't be working for Betty! The moral fiber of a woman who washes her nylon stockings in the bathroom sink and hangs them over the bathtub to dry.

While I have vast experience in the hand-cleaning habits of the male of the species, I'm not sure about the hand-cleaning habits of women. I suspect it takes several more minutes for a woman with long nails to wash her hands and even longer if the nails are glued on. I'm sure the devastation of an unclean nail has far-reaching consequences, but one broken while washing the hands is probably the ultimate setback. Extreme caution is, no doubt, required.

We can learn a lot from our medical professionals about keeping the hands clean. There's not a surgeon or nurse around who steps into the operating room without a good scrub first. I remember an old Three Stooges skit in which the Stooges played surgeons (You can't get too hung up on Three Stooges plots.) Moe scrubbed his hands, held them up in front of himself, and declared "Don't touch me, I'm sterile!" Now the sterility comment went over my head as a kid, but my Mom would always say, "See, kids, even a dumb man like Moe washes his hands." And they say you can't learn anything from television . . .

The ultimate in hand cleaning and its associated hygiene probably rests with the dentist. As a child, I recall Dr. Albertelli washing his hands and then plunging them into my mouth, prying my cheeks open as wide as the skin could tolerate. Running his fingers along every tooth. Flipping my lips up and feeling along my gums. It took a week for my face to return to its original shape. But, I could trust that these were clean hands invading my mouth. Today's dentists go even further. They wash up and then slap on a pair of rubber gloves and a mask. No germs trade homes from one person to another in today's dental chair.

And the moral of this story? Well, there isn't one really. If you wanna live like your ancestors, don't wash your hands. Heck, don't bathe either—that was a once-a-week endeavor up until a hundred years ago anyhow. And spend a little time researching such historic factoids as why Turks only shake hands with their left hand. You might be inspired. Above all, remember that it's better to wash your hands than wring your hands. So go lather up!

Tree frogs don't like to sit too long for a photo shoot. So we filled the gap in this picture with a frog-shaped cookie jar and a tree in the background—voila, tree frog! Thank God, the real frogs weren't as big as the cookie jar. (Photo by Joe Paradis).

Two Cents, 6-08-06

Matching Wits With a Tree Frog

I am, in general, a lover of nature. Oh, I don't hug trees, but I like to plant them. And I don't have a desire to live among the gorillas of Central Africa, but I like to pet every dog I pass. And when it comes to tree frogs, I am an absolute lover of the little guys, except that their extremely loud calls to one another—all night long and just ten feet from my window—drove my family crazy last summer. Like the family you love, but just can't live with. So I relocated a colony of those tree frogs from my swimming pool to a treed lot miles away, when we just couldn't take the piercing sound any longer. We still write to one another, exchange gifts at the holidays. I know they're safe and happy, because I heard them chirping away on that lot a week after their forced relocation. And the balance of nature was not harmed by my actions, so help me, Your Honor.

It's been occurring every night, just like clockwork, since the warm weather began. A shrill, piercing warble from somewhere out in the woods, behind our backyard. A sound so loud you would think the animal—whatever it is—is sitting on your shoulder.

And last night was no exception. The first series of shrieks was soon answered by that of another similar animal, somewhere else in the yard. And thus the nightly ritual began. An annoying back-and-forth "conversation" between two monsters determined to drive us out of our minds. A ritual that would continue for hours, under the cover of night when we would have no chance at all of locating them . . . and stomping their brains out.

Last Friday, the ritual began as usual and a roomful of us paused the TV after an hour of this pain, to analyze the situation.

"I think it's some kind of bird," said one of the kids.

"Could be," I responded. "But they aren't moving around. Birds don't stay in the same spot for hours, do they? Maybe it's an owl."

"Naw, owls hoot," offered another of the cherubs. "That's not a hoot. Maybe it's a mockingbird."

"Or a whippoorwill," chimed in another. "But don't they make a sound like their name?"

For a few moments, no other suggestions were offered.

"I think they're tree frogs," said Caitlin. Her words hung in the air like a thick summer mist. All conversation ceased.

"What was that?" I finally asked.

"Tree frogs," she repeated. "I think they're tree frogs."

A collective hum of approval issued from the crowd. "Tree frogs," I mused. "Could be, could be."

As far as I knew, we'd never had tree frogs in the yard. We'd never really experienced a summer sound any more annoying that the mild chirping of crickets, a sound that's at least tolerable. The question now before us was how to deal with this new irritant if, indeed, we were dealing with frogs. My son suggested a BB gun. Others suggested hand grenades, flamethrowers, strychnine. The problem was, of course, how to find a couple of frogs the size of a quarter, that were out there clinging to any one of a thousand trees under cover of darkness. An impossible task.

We turned the TV back on and endured those Godforsaken creatures for the next few hours, as fitting background sound for a movie called "Office Space." Then the party broke up and I went to bed, finally falling asleep, with the sound of those piercing shrieks bouncing around in my head.

The next day, as my wife and I took the cover off the pool, a couple of little frogs jumped onto the deck. I didn't think anything of it, just picked one of them up and placed him in the grass, so I wouldn't step on him. The other had already hopped away under the deck. Fifteen minutes later, we heard that familiar shrieking sound again—this time from under the deck. "Tree frogs . . . " I hissed, suddenly realizing my mistake. I ran out to the grass and found the little frog I'd placed there so gently. I released him into one of those plastic containers that our cherry tomatoes come in. It had plenty of little holes so he could breath. I put a little cup of water and a fistful of grass in the bottom and left him on the front porch. I would bring him to work the next morning and release him in the field to shriek as much as he wants—miles away from our house.

But I woke the next morning to find that he'd escaped. That wily tree bugger had wiggled through one of the bigger holes in the container and hopped off into our life again. I'd been beaten by a tree frog.

That evening, the familiar screeching sounds began again and I went frog hunting. I sat in the dark on the deck and followed their back-and-forth conversations until I could pinpoint their locations. Within a half hour, I'd caught three of them, all perched around the pool, sitting on the edge or clinging to the side. I retrieved a more secure plastic container from the recycle bin and put them in it. I then put that container in a carton and closed the cover. They weren't gonna get away this time... it was off to the Tree Frog Gulag for those three in the morning, where they could shriek to their heart's content, in a field far away from our home.

I reflected on the nerve of these noisy little creatures, who had apparently decided that our pool was their own private pond. It takes a lot of gall to invade someone's pool like that, especially if you're only an inch tall. But, I think I'd just shown three of them that it was MY pool, not theirs. They shrieked away in their plastic prison on the front porch. Keep screeching, you losers.

But there's still one frog out there that I couldn't find, shrieking as loudly as ever. He's still speaking to other frogs in the area, and I can hear their faint responses even though they're far away. But you know how these frogs are—first they find out that your house has a pool. Then they bring over a few dinner bugs, tell their friends about the place ... and next thing you know, they've built a commune around your yard. And you never, ever find restful sleep again.

So, you can bet I'll be out there again tomorrow night, circling the pool with my flashlight and my net. Oh, yeah—I'll eventually get that last little shrieker. Before he gets to me. And then all will be quiet in the yard once again. Until the crickets move back in. Or the in-laws come to visit.

If I know one fanatical barbeque guy, it is definitely my friend, Brian Southmayd. Brian has more cookout equipment than shingles on his roof. And he brought almost all of it out on the lawn for this picture, right down to the mustard and relish jars. Only problem was, we couldn't get even 25% of his stuff in the picture. But we did capture that fancy hat ... and how about those legs, eh? (Photo by Joe Paradis).

Two Cents, 7-06-06

Barbeque Man

This story tells the tale of a fairly stereotypical part of the American Backyard Legacy—the guy who thinks he's the ultimate outdoor chef. The Barbeque Man. He could be your father, your husband, your brother, your son. Or just an obnoxious neighbor whom you exploit for his cooking skills. He might really know what he's doing around that grill or perhaps he just has all the best equipment, with no idea of how to use it. Either way, this Bud's for you, bud!

Man and his barbeque. The American dream. Instant karma for the grillmeister. I'm not sure if there is any other pursuit around the house that a man finds to be more his domain than the five square feet around his barbeque grill. His lawn may be a distant second, because caring for that is a chore. But his barbecue isn't. It's an art. A loving ritual. An opportunity to create. And have you noticed, it's always "his" grill? A personal kingdom where he rules over forks and tongs; spices and marinades; plates of meat, vegetables, and seafood. All saluting him as the skipper of this ship.

In olden days, this master chef would often wear a heavy-duty apron, always white and emblazoned with some witty title, such as "King of the Grill" or "The Real Cook"—usually in green and red lettering. The daring one among them might also have the tall, matching chef's hat. He would proudly promenade this silly get-up at grillside, but never be caught wearing either of these items outside the confines of his own backyard, lest he be challenged on the street by a stevedore. Or a little old lady with attitude.

Now, it might be a stretch to always call this guy a chef. Sometimes he's just a regular Joe, who can barely grill a cheeseburger. But, standing there in front of his grill, sporting a can of Bud Lite and a Hawaiian shirt, opened to expose his ample gut, even the most earthy guy remains the man in charge of the food. And that's Status.

But the expert barbeque guy? Well, he's another story entirely. A true professional, he knows how to grill food to perfection. He understands that the careless application of flame can make or break a filet mignon. Or turn a tender chicken breast into a rubber chew toy. Or a cheeseburger into a hockey puck. He's as comfortable at the grill as he is at his job. And he's versatile—as easily able to fry up a 20-lb. turkey in the deep fryer, as he is to skewer kabobs or grill shrimp the old fashioned way.

The tools of his trade are generally encased in a plastic valise that he guards with his life. It contains his long-handled knife and fork. His tongs, skewers, and wire brush grill cleaner. And his flagship utensil, the spatula—also known as "that flipper thing" by the less sophisticated among us. His utensils are impeccably clean, even while he uses them.

He will brush vegetable oil on the grill before cooking and be certain to leave the flame on for a while after he has finished grilling—just to ensure that the leftover marinades are burned off the grill. He prepares and cooks his food "just so." Meat is timed, so that both sides receive equal exposure to the flame. Vegetables are cooked in tinfoil and must be properly seasoned and properly packaged. The curious should contain themselves and avoid trying to open these tinfoil packets before he has cooked them. It throws his entire day off. When not using his grill, he covers it with not one, but two official, and appropriately-sized, grill covers. He can be anal about these things.

He does not suffer cheap grills graciously. He would not own a Charbroil these days. Any grill with lava rocks or charcoal would be turned away, without remorse. He prefers a Weber or Vermont Castings grill. A stainless steel unit would make him drool, maybe bring a tear to his eye. But he's just as content with a combination stainless steel/cast iron grill—well... almost. He demands a grill with multiple heating zones and a Teflon-coated or aluminum grill top. The more side trays, shelves and storage areas, the better. He could care less about certain accessories, such as the optional gas burner. He believes that foods requiring a pan should be cooked on the stove, within the confines of his wife's kitchen. He admits that is her domain; she grants that the grill is his.

In his real life, he is a butcher, a baker, a candlestick maker. Or maybe an accountant. But on his backyard deck, there is none so manly as he who has perfected the art of the barbeque. Or so thinks he who barbeques.

And me? I have no pride of ownership to "my" grill. I'm trying to teach everyone in my house how to barbeque. Builds character. And scar tissue. It's a bit of a culture shock for most of them, but they are getting the hang of it. None of us will be deep frying turkeys anytime soon though. For that, we'll be eating over the professional's house. Ya gotta know how far to push these things . . .

There are some informal rules for Guys Night Out. You need at least four guys and ... well that's about it. Here, four of America's Finest get ready for a night out. After pooling their resources, the night out amounted to a cheap meal at a Mexican restaurant. (Photo by Joe Paradis).

Two Cents, 7-27-06

Guys Night Out

In my younger days, I always had a night out with the boys. Every Saturday night, as a matter of fact. With about a dozen of the guys. Of course, none of us was married then, so no one was holding us back or glaring at us, as we left our homes for the evening. Except maybe our mothers—most of us still lived with our parents. As I matured—if you can call it that—I was less interested in a night out with the boys. We had all gone our separate ways anyhow to raise families and join the rat race. So when I do get the rare chance to step out these days, I'm pretty much lost. As you will see . . .

In my house, there's really no such thing as a "guys night out." Oh, sure, there's a "ladies night out" for my wife. That usually consists of something like a monthly movie with the Red Hatters, lunch with a friend, or, on a rare occasion, dinner with the girls after work. These "ladies nights out" usually last all of two hours tops. Safe nights out that most husbands can tolerate, without feeling jealous.

But as far as Joe goes, "guys night out" has pretty much been a foreign concept for these past 22 years of marriage. After all, where do guys typically go during a guys night out? Some smoky barroom? A pool hall? The more rambunctious or foolhardy might head to a "gentlemen's club." I'm not really keen on any of those places, being the faithfully-married guy that I am. But either way, unlike the girls night out, a guys night out wouldn't exactly consist of going out together for dinner at the 99. Or lunch. And there's something odd about a bunch of guys going to the movies together, at least in my book.

Realistically, night out options are fairly limited for guys who are a.) happily married, b.) light drinkers, c.) wearers of the marital ball & chain, or d.) all of the above. That's why many of us who fall into one or another of those categories tend to also have hobbies like stamp collecting, building models, or playing chess. And chances are good, most of us don't dance very well.

But once in awhile, we homeboys are allowed to venture out with "the guys." To let our proverbial hair down. Maybe pop a "one-cheek sneak" in public and be roundly praised by our compadres for the sound and texture of that effort. To do manly things that aren't real manly, but that don't land us in trouble either. Such an opportunity arises for me every summer when my industry holds its annual convention in some faraway exotic location. Okay, so it was only Boston this year. Well, for the last few. Except for a year ago, when it was held in Philadelphia. Which is like Boston with more people. How exotic is that, eh?

So last week I headed south for two days in Boston. I was even able to find my way to the hotel. Once there, I did what every wild and crazy guy does—found the hotel restaurant and ate like a pig. Well, not really a pig, but like a guy using his company expense account. Eating deeply, I guess you'd call it. Then I went back to my room, called home, watched the rest of the Sox game, and fell asleep. So much for Night #1 of "guys night out."

Night #2 was where the action was—or as much action as I could stand. We began with dinner in the downstairs dining room of a famous Italian restaurant in Boston's North End, compliments of one of our vendors. Once a solid backbone of Boston's Italian community, the North End is now also home to way too many yuppies yearning to experience the joys of living in a 'flat' surrounded by the smells of neighborhood bakeries and the frustration of too few parking spaces. We missed all that ambiance, as we pulled up to the restaurant in a fleet of cabs. We had the basement dining area to ourselves, in a room adjacent to the wine collection. One might question the wisdom of seating a bunch of guys that close to thousands of dollars worth of wine, but there were none of those heavy drinking types in this crowd. And besides, this was still the North End where people are more inclined to behave. Or else.

One of the best dinners I've had in a long time was accompanied by great conversation and a special treat. A wine tasting. Three wines at a time, nine total samples, served with our meal. A roving wine expert circulated around the room, telling us the history of the grapes, the region they were from. He spoke of full-bodied wine, aroma, and bouquet. He was very informative—I had no idea what he was talking about.

Now, in my experience with wine tastings like this, I find that people do a lot of nodding—as if they actually understand what the vintner is saying. They swirl their wine because everybody else does, inhale deeply over the glass, swish the wine in their mouths. These are guys whose preferred beverage is usually Bud Lite. In reality, few of them could actually differentiate a wine's bouquet from a spring bouquet, let alone detect a hint of cherry or a nutty flavor. But they're fun to watch—and this crowd was no exception.

After dinner, a dozen of us waddled down the street to a cigar bar. A throwback to the smoky gentlemen's parlors of the 1800s, where only the men would gather to enjoy a cigar and a brandy, this cigar bar had a bit of that era's ambiance. Heavy red drapes were tied back to reveal cozy little nooks all along the wall. I half expected to see politicians in seedy suits making backroom deals in these cozy settings. But, of course that was impossible—you couldn't see anything through the haze of cigar smoke. We all selected cigars from the menu. I knew less about cigars than I did about wine, so I said "I'll have the same" when the guy next to me ordered. I was soon presented with a cigar the size of a flagpole, which the waitress lit with a flamethrower. And we all sat around and puffed those stogies until we just couldn't take the thick air anymore. Which was about an hour.

We then hailed cabs back to our hotel. On the way, I had a great conversation with our cab driver, an affable, illegal alien from Haiti—a story unto itself. We didn't know whether to report him or give him a larger tip. We settled for the tip—this was, after all, Boston, declared a haven for illegal aliens by the mayor, just last year. Our cab driver might have received the key to the city had we ratted on him.

And that, my friends, was my "guys night out" for this year. Nothing fancy. Just a little bonding time with the guys. Maybe next year, we'll jazz it up a bit. Perhaps we'll find a Turkish Hookah bar, eat some Greek food. Maybe talk it up with two or three illegal aliens. I can't wait. In the meantime, pass me my stamp collection, will ya? I need to calm down.

Ah, the in-ground swimming pool. Always a serene setting before the "big party," when even the pool starts to feel its age. (Photo by Joe Paradis).

Two Cents, 8-03-06

The Family Pool Party, Part I.

God knows if I'll ever write a novel. Maybe someday. I understand it's much more difficult than just writing the short stories that I typically do. They say you need to design a plot, lay out a story, concoct characters, do some research. I've never been sure if I'd be up to all that. Then I read Stephen King's book "On Writing." Essentially King just goes at it—he writes and lets it flow. So I tried that too with this story—just to see if I could write something that I could build on and maybe turn into a longer book. I never got to a Part II. Not yet anyhow. But I had a lot of fun building these characters and at least giving it a shot.

It was the worst kind of summer day. Ninety-four degrees; eighty percent humidity. A thick haze hung over everything, with the constant threat of a thundershower that just never came. You could cut the air with a knife and another sponge of muggy dew would immediately hit you in the face. There was no relief whatsoever.

And on that fetid Sunday afternoon in August, Bob and Myrtle decided to risk their lives and their neighborhood reputation, by doing something they rarely ever did. They invited the family over for a pool party.

The gathering was certainly overdue, they readily admitted. After all, they hadn't seen most of the family in over a year. Not since the Fourth of July cookout at Cousin Fred's condo, when Uncle Jasper burned down the garage with his fireworks display. But the insurance company had paid off on the claim, cousin Fred's hair had grown back, and time must have healed all wounds. Or so they hoped. So Bob and Myrtle decided that this mid-summer party would be just the thing to meld the family into one big happy brood again. If, indeed, they ever really were one big happy brood.

Myrtle had spent the last three days preparing the food. She'd marinated chicken wings, steak tips, and shrimp for the grill. She made potato salad, pasta salad, Caesar salad, and fruit salad. She even bought those little chicken gizzards and a pound of tripe for Grandpa. Bob had done what he does best—cleaned the grill and the pool, mowed the lawn, and bought beer and ice. He did it all on Saturday morning and in the afternoon, sampled the beer, to ensure it's freshness, as he watched the ballgame on ESPN. His was a Machiavellian life.

By 10 a.m. the next morning, Bob was ready to greet their guests. Myrtle was ready for a nap. Both of them stood watch on the front porch, waiting for the cars to appear. "Maybe they'll leave early," Myrtle wished out loud.

"Maybe they'll get lost on the way," hoped Bob. Fat chance, he admitted afterwards. This crowd hadn't missed a meal in years. Not since 1998, when Bob's brother Paul threw up on the little plastic bride and groom on the top of his wedding cake. A bad omen for him. And a raw deal for the family. They didn't get dessert that day . . .

But both Bob and Myrtle knew that the family would indeed arrive today. Most, after all, were coming from the city, where the temperature had exceeded 98 degrees every day last week. They would all be looking forward to a nice day in the countryside with their favorite country relatives, Bob and Myrtle Shmirnov.

So, Bob and Myrtle braced for the onslaught, and only they knew the tension that ripped through their hearts, as they bravely smiled and waived, when the first three cars pulled into the driveway.

Bob's brother Paul was driving the first car. He got out, stretching mightily, and rubbed his huge belly, which hung over the edge of his bathing suit like the White Cliffs of Dover overhang the English Channel. Two deep belches later, after a quick rearranging of his comb-over, Bob unlocked the rear door, and his four small boys, aged six to ten, poured out. Dressed to kill in their camouflaged bathing suits, each one was touting a Super Soaker squirt rifle and yelling at the top of his lungs.

"Run on up and drench your Uncle Bob, boys. He doesn't look wet enough," Paul said, chuckling.

His third wife Lisa laughed heartily, as the boys scrambled up the stairs. Uncle Bob never had a chance. "Oh, Paul . . . " she said, sweating profusely, as she adjusted her bright yellow tank top, pulling it down over a belly that equaled her husband's. "You're so mean to your brother. Let the boys grab a few cheeseburgers before they play with him."

They both laughed as they grabbed the donuts and Cheese Doodles off the front seat, and waddled together up the walkway. "Come on, guys," Paul yelled over his shoulder, as all doors to the two vehicles behind him opened in a mad rush. His oldest son Joshua and Josh's new girlfriend, Melody, were the first to dismount.

"Cool place," said Melody, as she surveyed Myrtle's summer gardens and the huge farmer's porch. She tossed her cigarette butt in the flowerbed, smoothed down her leather vest, and pulled a pair of sunglasses off her long, greasy, orange and purple hair.

"I love it here!" Joshua replied. He himself was dressed in his best Gothic Grungewear, right down to the twelve matching earrings, one that ran through front of his nose and another through his bottom lip. "Let's go show Auntie Myrtle your new tattoo! She's a forensic cop—she'll probably get a charge out of the skull and crossbones!" And they too scampered up the walkway, close on the heals of Josh's dad.

Meanwhile, Grandma and Grandpa were having a tough time getting out of the third car. Grandma's moo-moo had gotten stuck in the door and she hadn't realized it, as she excitedly headed for the walkway, calling out "Bobby! Bobby, my little boy! Come kiss your mother." The result was a huge rip in her dress and a mighty tug backwards that knocked her floppy hat off her head.

"Foolish woman . . . " Grandpa muttered under his breath, as he crushed his cigar out on the driveway, and ambled around to assist his wife. He was forever having to save her from these self-induced mishaps. "You gotta be careful, Ester. It's too late in the season to find another one of those moo-moos at WalMart."

"I'm sorry, Sal," said the slight woman. "I'm just so excited to be seeing the kids again. Do you think Mary can sew the rip?"

"Yeah, maybe . . . if you call her by her right name. It's Myrtle, not Mary. She's only been married to Bob for ten years."

"Oh, that's right."

"What the hell are you too arguing about?" bellowed Uncle Jasper from the back seat. "Let's get this show on the road. I'm hungry." He scrambled out of the car and stood there, hands on hips; a scrawny, little man in plaid shorts, black socks and sandals. Thin blue stripes zipped across his yellow imitation Polo shirt. With his Panama Jack hat and oversized sunglasses, he looked a bit like a skinny Truman Capote.

"Let's get up there now, before the rest of the gang arrives. You know how they are around food." Ester and Sal indeed knew that scenario. Sal dislodged his wife's moo-moo from the doorjam, covered the rip as best he could, and escorted her up the walkway. Uncle Jasper followed, slightly nudging his frail sister ahead of him. He and Ester were the two 'featherweights' of the family.

Myrtle surveyed all of this from her beautiful farmer's porch, while Bob was busy dodging squirt gun blasts from his nephews. She was suddenly terrified that perhaps they had made a mistake with this party. But she took a deep breath as the first adult guests started to climb the stairway, knowing that, not far behind them was another band of relatives that made this group seem tame...

Two Cents, 8-24-06

When the Boys Come to Call

The ultimate dilemma facing every father who has a daughter is boys. We want to know whom she dates, when she dates, what the kid is like, everything about him before they even leave the front porch together. We want to meet his parents, approve of his clothing, check out his CD collection—just to make sure he's good enough for our daughters. Ultimately, he isn't. He's either way too different from us—or way too similar. We know all his motives; we were there once too. When our daughters ask what time they should be home, we say 9 o'clock. Then we stare at the boyfriend and dare him to say differently. He never does. But we concede to letting them stay out till 11 o'clock and then follow them down to his car. They'll be back at 11; we know that. Because if they aren't, fathers have "options" . . .

We were at the dinner table the other night. Just three of us—my wife, my son, and I. My daughter was upstairs preparing for one of those "dates with a friend." Such friend dates usually consist of a movie or miniature golf, maybe an ice cream. Sometimes, even dinner at the 99. They always involve a girl and a boy—most often splitting the bill.

Personally, I think the boy should always pay for these dates, even if the kids are just friends. But the old rules of etiquette aren't very compatible with today's social definition of what constitutes a date, so that's wishful thinking on my part. Still and all, a "date with a friend" appears to be a safe kind of date, with the girl usually home by 10 p.m. At least in my house.

Now when the boy decides that his interest in the girl has deepened and wants to be "more than friends"—that's when the daddy in me gets a lot more defensive. Let's be realistic, there aren't many boys who just want to be friends with a girl, particularly when they are sixteen years old. All dads know that—we were, after all, once sixteen ourselves.

These thoughts whirled around in my feeble mind as we sat down to dinner. "Do we know this kid?" I finally asked my wife and son. My daughter was at the front window, still watching for her friend.

It's a fantasy, to be sure. But my son and I thought it would be fun to portray the type of characters I envisioned in this story. (Photo by Danielle Paradis).

"I don't think we've met him," my wife replied. "He's a senior at the high school. They've been IM-ing each other."

"Oh," I said. Silence settled in for awhile. We could hear the crunching sound of each other's teeth, as we bit into our corn on the cob. I finished first, and wiped my mouth. "You know, I've always wanted to ask these kids, when they come to the door, what their intentions are with my daughter," I mused.

"Good one, Dad," my son said. He prefers to greet these kids at the door with his shirt off (he's been working out a little these days) and one of his knife sheathings strapped to his belt. His high-and-tight haircut completes a visual image of the big brother concerned for his little sister. And he never smiles at them. Good acting for a kid who's generally pretty congenial.

I continued. "Yeah, I could say something like 'are you the pizza guy?' and when he says 'no', I could just close the door in his face." My son started to chuckle.

"Or I could say 'I'm glad you're here. I didn't get my *Watchtower* magazine last month. Did you bring it this time?" Jehovah's Witnesses had been a friendly staple at our door for years. That scenario had both of us laughing.

"Or maybe I could just yell in from the other room as if I was drunk, slurring something like 'C'mon in. The doors open,' in a loud bellowing voice." By now, my son and I were laughing wildly at our own outrageous wit.

I thought of other scenarios. How it might be cool to just sit on the front porch, cleaning my shotgun when one of these kids arrived. Sort of the Appalachian Mountain Man approach. Or maybe I could greet the next kid at the door with my chainsaw in hand, as if I was just heading out to fell a few trees. That would be the Canadian lumberjack approach. But after looking at my wife, I refrained from expressing any more of my ideas. She just sat there rolling her eyes, as my son and I both convulsed with laughter. She wasn't as impressed with our dim wit as we were.

My daughter took this all in stride, knowing (or so she hoped) that we were kidding. She kept glancing out the front window, watching for the arrival of her friend. And I ran through the scenarios again. I was just finishing up the drunk guy scenario, when my daughter's friend came through the door. Having been caught acting like a fool, I did what any dad would do. I stood and introduced myself. "How are you? I'm Mr. Paradis, Danielle's dad." My wife did the same. My son remained seated, shirtless, and turned around to shake hands, a somber look on his face.

We exchanged about twenty more words among us and the two kids headed off to the miniature golf course.

I have to say it's a lot more difficult on a father when it's his daughter, rather than his son, who's going on these dates. Guess I'll just have to dream up a few more of those introduction scenarios—and maybe start using them seriously . . .

It was truly an interesting harvest that season. Even the Vigaro didn't help. But I could proudly display the results on a platter, at any rate—with a bit of garnish. (Photo by Joe Paradis).

Two Cents, 11-09-06

A Bountiful Harvest

Ever since I was a kid, I've always grown a vegetable garden. At the very least, tomatoes and cukes. Sometimes I'd get exotic. One year, I planted Jerusalem artichokes. They aren't what you'd expect. The Jerusalem artichoke is a tuber crop—like potatoes. And for two years after I planted them, they sprouted all throughout my Dad's lawn. Not my finest moment—or his either, for that matter. But I've always loved planting a bountiful vegetable garden. Except for last year ...

The fall harvest is upon us, folks. Alas, for home gardeners like I, that means it's time to bring in the last of those fresh garden vegetables, turn the soil, and wait it out till next spring. It's also time to brace for a winter of chewing through those rubbery carrots, tasteless tomatoes, and thick-skinned cucumbers available in supermarkets everywhere.

When we first moved to New Hampshire 24 years ago, I was really gung ho on vegetable gardening. Finally, I would have enough land to plant a real garden! I began by laying out a plot 40 feet by 60 feet—right over the leach field, of course. I grew everything from seed, which I purchased only through mail order catalogs. I planted tomatoes, cukes, peppers, lettuce, eggplant, and zucchini. Peas, carrots, string beans, pumpkins and gourds. Also summer squash, winter squash, acorn squash, butternut squash, hubbard squash (we like squash). Big food, big plans.

In February, I would germinate the seeds under grow lamps in our basement, which consumed half the area—even the tops of the washing machine and dryer. In March, I'd move about eight billion seedlings to my greenhouse, which I built myself, and installed passive solar heating to keep my babies warm. In May, I'd turn all the rows in my garden by hand. I had always wanted one of those TroyBuilt tillers and would drool over their brochures year after year. But, alas, that purchase was never to be—we had kids instead. On May 11, I would plant, because that was the last official day of frost for New Hampshire. Once in awhile, we'd have a late frost after that date and I'd run out with newspaper to cover all the plants. Yep, I was a regular, dedicated, Mr. Green Jeans farmer in those days . . .

But, the sadness and reality of yet another year's harvest brings me back to last spring, when, once again, I just couldn't wait to get outside and spread manure over my now much-reduced 12' x 16' garden plot. It wasn't the manure that excited me—just the fact that spring was back and I could start planting. Frankly, I'm not really into manure the way some folks are. I know certain manure aficionados who tout the wonders of fresh chicken manure over the more traditional cow manure. Others rave about the firmness of horse manure. And there's always one sheep guy in the crowd. As I understand it, some people in France are even into human manure—but for reasons that have nothing to do with gardening. Personally, I go with the dehydrated cow manure that comes in a bag at Home Depot. It has no poopie odor, so the yard doesn't smell as if the septic tank backed up. But enough about manure; I could just go on forever . . .

My point here is that, while my garden and ambition have shrunk considerably over the years, I was still excited to go through the annual rituals of gardening last spring. To comb through the wide varieties of tomatoes, cukes, zucchini, and summer squash—now purchased at the local nursery—and still, in the end, select the same plants that I do every year. To turn the good soil, dig my holes, and plant those little babies in the ground. Seeds are out, potted plants are in. Convenience, not hard work, is now the name of the vegetable gardening game for me.

I even splurged this year and installed a drip irrigation system that was supposed to conserve water, as it only feeds to the soaker hoses that run by each vegetable plant. The system looked perfect on the box it came in. I bought two. It was also supposed to save a lot of water over the old oscillating sprinkler I'd used in the past—although, without the overspray from the sprinkler, my driveway wasn't nearly as clean this year. In the end, the plants never really got enough water; and I pulled out the old oscillating sprinkler. So much for buying something by looking at the picture on the box.

However, I was still psyched for a bountiful harvest throughout the summer and into the fall and everything started out beautifully. By summer, my gardens usually run themselves—with minimal care.

A few weeks ago, I brought in the harvest. One single tomato. Really. Oh, I was also fortunate enough to salvage a few handfuls of parsley, but that comes up every year.

I'm not sure what happened to the crops this year. There weren't any bugs or grubs, or cutworms. A couple of slugs popped up, as did a fat gopher who visited daily to nibble at the few veggies that did grow out. But he wasn't getting fat off this sad bunch of plants. Maybe some strain of Asian Vegetable Blight had reached our shores off a ship unloading its Chinese cargo in Portsmouth Harbor. Or maybe acid rain was concentrating this year right over my garden. Perhaps, unknown to me, my little plot had been declared a hazardous waste site. We've had a few of those in town over the years.

It could have been aliens. Or maybe, just maybe, the manure aficionados were right about their distain for my dehydrated cow poop. I'll check with the French.

Whatever the reason, I'll not be deterred. I'm still gonna launch into another garden next spring, as I do every year . . . 'cause that was still one tasty, little tomato. And with just one cuke, I could've had a salad.

So many questions in the bathroom . . . Seat up or seat down? Toilet paper rolled over the top or underneath? Where do <u>you</u> stand on these important issues? (Photo by Joe Paradis).

Two Cents, 11-16-06

The Great Bathroom Debates

I'd always thought that writing about "potty things" would make for a funny story. But I also knew it had to be somewhat "tasteful"—if that's the word. After all, I have a lot of prim and proper readers who don't appreciate potty talk. So I wrote this story. And for weeks later, I had so many people tell me their preference for leaving the seat up or down, rolling the toilet paper from the top or the bottom, and the general condition of the soap in their showers, that I felt I'd struck the right chord. Except for one older woman who sent me a lovely flowered card, telling me that she generally loved my stories, but was truly disgusted with this one. I hope she's forgiven me. This creative writing sure can be a dirty business . . .

In the wake of recent elections, always a nasty business, it's probably appropriate for us to examine the serious concerns which emanate from the most utilized room in the house—the bathroom. To that end, I present to you my Top Ten Bathroom Debates, may God save my soul.

1. Seat up or seat down. This is the ultimate bathroom argument between women and men. Guys generally keep the seat up, ladies like it down. As a guy, I'd like to say that we keep the seat up out of concern for the women of the household. Picture any guy rushing in from raking the leaves who's just gotta "go." If the seat is up, he can't splash it, avoiding an uncomfortable situation for his wife next time she uses the facilities. If it's down, let's face it, few guys are going to run a sheet of toilet paper over the seat afterwards. No guy is going to admit that his aim is that poor.
2. Toilet paper—rolled over or under. I believe this preferential trait is a learned reaction from one's mother. Personally, I prefer my TP rolled over the top. Makes it easier to spin a few feet of paper out for quick access. As a kid, I used to see how closely I could roll the paper to the floor with one spin, without the TP actually touching the floor. It's a skill that can

only be mastered with the TP rolled over the top. For those who roll their toilet paper under . . . I see no hope.

3. When to replace the soap. Soap is obviously the mainstay of the shower. The Great Soap Debate has always been: when is the bar too small to use. My dad would use a bar until it broke into so many small pieces that he could no longer squeeze them into a ball. I've developed that habit too, but my wife has a different perspective. Which is why she leaves a fresh bar on the side of the sink, in its opened box, as a hint, when she thinks I should change the bar after my shower. Being a guy, I usually forget—magically, I have a new bar to work with the next day anyhow.

4. Flushing. We all recall some young child in his or her first year of responsible potty use, who forgets to flush, leaving . . . well, what often looks like a Baby Ruth candy bar floating on the surface of the toilet bowl. We're usually accepting of this oversight in young children. But, to all the wives and moms out there, if the water in your toilet is a deep yellow color, or in the case of those who use the "blue water," a deep green color, you need to have a conversation with the men in your household. Someone's not following through.

5. Clogging the drain. I'm amazed at how often my wife tells me that the water is draining slowly in the bathroom sink. I really don't think it's because the tooth paste doesn't dissolve or because the hair from the cats, who love to sit in the sink, suddenly creates a fur ball in the drainpipe. Instead, I suspect those gobs of foot-long hairs, held together by soap scum, may come from a female suspect or two in my own household, who spend hours each week drying their hair over the sink. This is just a hunch.

6. A wet bathroom rug. There is a raging debate as to whether the bathroom rug, so neatly positioned in front of the tub, is really meant to be stepped on with wet feet. I was raised to dry off each foot before stepping out of the tub and on to the rug. Others say that the rug is there for exactly that purpose—to soak up the water from their feet. Of course, these folks are usually the first to use the tub each morning,

so they've never suffered the joy of stepping into a swamp left by the previous bather.

7. A cold toilet seat. Few household experiences are as bone chilling as having to sit on a cold toilet seat when you really have to "go" at two o'clock in the morning. It's the posterior equivalent of a "brain freeze" from eating ice cream too quickly. I'm sure some entrepreneur out there is working on a heated toilet seat, similar to the heated seats in luxury cars. Just beware of an electric current running through a seat so close to the water in your toilet bowl. That's called an electric chair.

8. Air freshener. The mainstay of any room established exclusively for the purpose of passing gas, a can of air freshener is a "must have" in any bathroom. It's just rude not to have it available. In my house we've found the chemical reaction of Oust to be a pleasant experience. My sister calls it Oost, but maybe that's just a language barrier thing. We have, of course, tried other brands, but somehow a scent like "Spring Bouquet" just doesn't mix well with sewage gas, no matter how much of it you dump (poor choice of words) into the air.

9. Reading materials. Every quality bathroom has a decent selection of reading materials, constantly rotated to provide hours of reading enjoyment, if that proves to be needed. Avoid bathrooms that have none—you can only read the ingredients of the air freshener can so many times. Take your business elsewhere.

10. Wiping the shower walls. It's a pretty sure bet that those who wipe down the tub and the walls after their shower spend less time later trying to scrub layers of soap scum off them. Imagine if you didn't wipe other things that you normally do in a bathroom. Enough said on that—grab a sponge, pardner, and start wiping.

So there you have it—my list of the Top Ten Bathroom Debates, in no particular order. I hope society will finally deal with these dysfunctional discussions, so that someday we can flush the whole thing down the toilet, once and for all.

Stringing the Christmas lights year after year can be a chore. In this picture, even Santa looks weary. (Photo by Joe Paradis).

Two Cents, 12-07-06

Another Year of Stringing the Lights

I love Christmas—but really more so for the joy of the season, rather than all the hoopla of buying predominantly useless gifts for everyone in our address book. Oh, I do like to decorate the house—but only with white lights and not so the place looks like a disco dance floor. That just gets to be too such to maintain—especially when one string of lights goes out in the middle of an ice storm. You need to fix that—otherwise your decorations don't look very festive. And, of course, what would the neighbors think? Stay with me on this one...

"Don't wanna," I said, but not too firmly. I knew the inevitability of the situation.

"Why not?" my wife responded. "It's a beautiful day, perfect weather. There won't be many more days like this before Christmas."

She was right and I knew it. It was sixty degrees outside. So with a heavy sigh, I trudged up the second-floor stairs and retrieved the outdoor Christmas decorations from the closet. We don't have many outside decorations left—only five or six cartons these days. I'm gradually working to get that down to zero cartons. Well...maybe one. Okay, maybe two. We'll see...

Toward that end, I try to toss out something each year. Last year, I threw out our tacky lights in the shape of bows, which we had always strung across the porch railings. Every single year, there was always one section of bulbs on those monsters that wouldn't light. It required a painstaking search for the one loose bulb that was preventing electricity from flowing. To address that problem, I've always used the fairly reliable "shake method," recommended by 3 out of 4 cogent Christmas decorators. This involves a sharp shake or two to the problem area. With a little luck, that's usually enough to jolt the lights on. But if the shake doesn't work or just loosens more bulbs—and if, like me, you haven't the patience to check every bulb to see which are loose—then, again like me, you just toss the darned thing in the trash. So that's what I did last year. I am positive that one of our trash men is enjoying our bow lights this year—because he possesses the virtue of true patience which I lack.

But there was still plenty of stuff to use this year. I unpacked the fake garland, which still looks pretty realistic, and wound it around the six posts on the porch. I unpacked the huge, gold-painted, plastic ornaments and dangled those above the railings where the petunia plants hang in better weather. I hung the wreath on the front door and the made-in-Communist-China "Christmas Welcome" sign from the lamp post. That was it for the easy stuff.

Next, I unpacked, ever so gently, the icicle lights that we hang along the roof edge on the gutters. Thankfully this year, only one section of that thirty-foot length required the "shake method." They went up like a charm. So did the string of lights for the front of the greenhouse.

I wasn't as fortunate with the wire reindeer that we usually place on the front lawn. When I tested them in the garage, they lit up completely, all along the shape of the reindeer. Perfect, I thought. But somehow, once I had them firmly anchored into the lawn, exposure to the air or sunlight or the soil—or perhaps the shock of touch by human hands—caused only half of the lights to come on. And that's unacceptable; civilized people just don't display half-lit reindeer. I tried the "shake method" more times than I cared to, but to no avail. They just wouldn't light up. I thought briefly about using the more revolutionary "throw method," but couldn't bear myself to toss animals across the front lawn, even fake wire ones. PETA spies are everywhere, you know. So the reindeer will just sit on the lawn this year—anchored down well, but unlit. Looks like the trash man will get another bunch of Christmas decorations in the spring...

I made the precarious trip up onto the roof, to hang our large plastic wreath from the peak of the house. I was literally hanging over the edge of the peak, trying to find the hook, when the toot of a car horn almost sent me over the edge. I'm jittery enough on that roof; didn't really need any extra excitement at that particular moment. It turned out to be Anne, our friendly mail carrier, bringing a package up to the house. We had a nonchalant chat from afar, Anne acting as if she had conversations every day with people hanging over the edge of their roofs. She's a good girl; I hope her horn is broken in the spring, when I hit the roof again to take that wreath down.

I still had to coordinate our humble lighting display, so I took another hour to get all the timers synchronized. Nothing worse than a slipshod light display at Christmas, you know. I was quite pleased with myself, as darkness quickly descended upon me at 4 o'clock and all my timers clicked on simultaneously. I put away my sledgehammer, duct tape, and chainsaw (you never know what you'll encounter with Christmas decorations) and headed inside for a cup of coffee.

And so went the task of outside Christmas decorating for yet another year.

The next morning, I caught my wife out on the front porch, looking over the weeping cherry tree in front of the house. I smelled trouble. "You know," she said, "This tree would look great with Christmas lights on it."

"Yeah, so would you," I caught myself thinking. But I just smiled and nodded to my lovely bride, and we headed off to Church. I'm sure I'll be hanging those lights next weekend. Some chores are just never finished.

Girls will be girls. And their conversations are generally foreign to me. Here my sister Pat and her daughter Shayna exchange girl talk that was apparently crucial enough to require recording, courtesy of Terry, Shayna's mother-in-law. (Photo by Joe Paradis).

Two Cents, 3-22-07

Girl Talk

As a writer, I find it beneficial to be fairly observant. Observations are, after all, the source of many of my stories. Okay... call it eavesdropping. Nonetheless, there's always a time or two when I'm just caught off guard by some of the things I've "observed." This was one of those times—a conversation that took place right next to me as I was working. I tell ya, the things some guys are forced to endure...

The other day, I was sitting at my computer, putting a few final touches on my last article, when I heard someone say "I love your eyebrows." Now I've never been flattered by anyone for much of anything, so this was quite a shock. It did, in fact, caused me to raise an eyebrow. I stopped typing for just a moment.

"Do you really?" responded a second voice. I sighed audibly, quite relieved. Thank God, this wasn't a conversation with me or about me. It was merely two of the ladies in the office discussing something totally foreign to me—apparently the care and maintenance of one's eyebrows.

"Yes, I love them!" exclaimed the first woman. "They're so nice and even. I can never get mine to look like that."

"And see, they did my upper lip too. They took all the hair off." Now I was beginning to feel just a wee bit uncomfortable. This was the type of conversation I imagined takes place in the women's bathroom at a wedding reception. I resumed typing, even more furiously.

But they continued. A discussion that started at the eyebrows and traveled down the upper lip, now focused on chins and necks. I was witness to a fascinating conversation about a woman they know who had a "loose neck, one that ran from the bottom of her chin, straight down, to the bottom of her neck." Apparently, a family trait. And, this was, of course, the reason why she wore her hair long. I'd had about enough now. If they kept discussing body parts any lower than the chin, this could get really awkward. So I did the best thing I could to alleviate the pain of this conversation. I chimed in.

"Yeah, I know someone too with one of those necks!" I said. "She just wears turtle necks to cover things up. No big deal." They both looked at me for a second. I don't think it was the best icebreaker. But I thought it would save me further embarrassment. Then they broke out laughing and parted, hopefully to get back to the reason why we all go to work in the first place. I had escaped unscathed!

And that's the problem with girl talk. Guys don't understand it. It's like a foreign language to us. That's because we don't often stand around complimenting one another on our hygiene or personal habits. No guy has ever said to me "Nice shave today, Joe. Did you use a straight edge or an electric razor?" We just keep conversations like that at a manly distance—like about 300 miles. Or even 1,000.

But not the ladies! Girl talk rules. I just finished up a month-long training course at work. For every day of that course, at two-hour intervals, our female instructor would continue to lecture, while simultaneously applying hand cream AND lip balm to those particular areas of her body. Didn't miss a beat in her presentation. She even put cotton gloves on afterwards, apparently to retain the moisture, as she worked the overhead projector. It was, I must admit, a pretty smooth feat. But I couldn't picture most guys whipping out the skin lotion while giving a lecture. Except maybe a flamboyant one, here or there. Or maybe Dr. Phil.

Now in the interest of equal treatment, some ladies might readily admit that a few of the things they've caught guys doing aren't all that impressive either. One female friend was pretty disgusted with her husband's habit of extending his finger into his nostril as an alternative to using a handkerchief. Can't argue with that one. Another thought her boyfriend's habit of chewing on his fingernails was a bit nasty, particularly since he apparently gnaws on them with the greatest of gusto just as he's leaving his job as an auto mechanic. Can't argue with that one either. But I beg to offer a difference here. I don't think those guys stand around with other guys discussing these things. I'd even venture to say that they engage in most of those interesting habits while driving in their cars. Where, by the way, I've also seen women applying their eye liner while driving down the road at forty miles an hour. But that's not the kind of stuff I'm talking about here. I'm talking about pure girl talk, not rude habits. There is, to my mind, no male equivalent.

My older sister used to have an occasional girls' sleep over when we were kids. These were most frequent when she first entered high school. Even though I was younger, I liked to hang around them, because... well, they were girls and I was at that age when boys start getting interested in them. But I remember these girls all gathering on the living room rug, decked out in their pajamas and fuzzy slippers, to paint their nails, giggle, and engage in that evil girl talk. Despite my fascination with them, it wasn't pretty to listen to the discussion about nails and bra sizes and costume jewelry. The only satisfaction I got out of those sessions was a great picture I snapped of my sister in her giant can-sized hair rollers. I hid behind the couch for the perfect shot, and I used that picture as "leverage" for a number of years. Until she found it in my drawer and ripped it up. But I still have the negative. Wait till she hits fifty.

To this day, that early run in with girl talk probably accounts for my habit of cringing whenever a group of two or more women gathers near me and I hear the words "Oh, I just love your... (fill in the blank)." I know it's a scene I want to avoid. So I seek consolation in finding the nearest group of guys, who are usually talking about last night's football game or their cars, but never about their aftershave lotion or shoes. It's a tough world out there, guys. Tread lightly.

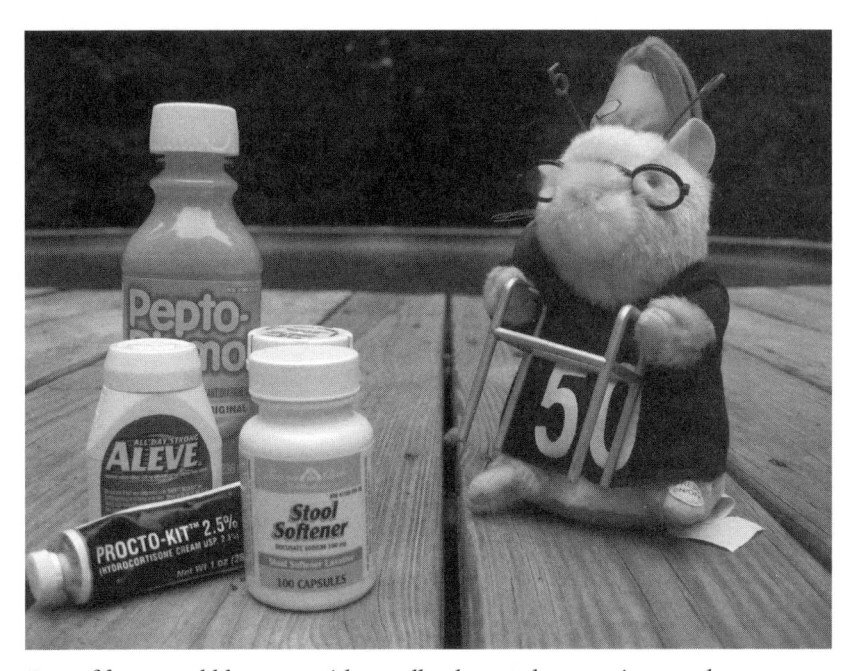

Every fifty-year-old hamster with a walker knows that certain over-the-counter drugs become medicine chest staples once you hit that milestone age. (Photo by Joe Paradis).

Two Cents, 7-29-04

Turning Fifty

People really seem to get their undies in a wedgy over aging, don't they? Especially as they reach those "milestone" birthdays like the 30th, 40th, and 50th. I'm not really sure why that is, although certainly the milestones provide us personal insight into our own mortality. When people reach that ripe old age of thirty, they are generally in the midst of building a career and a family. At 40, many are still doing that—and some have reached the peak earning years. At 50, I found that, while the body slowed down a bit, and it took me a wee bit longer to remember where I left my shoes, I was generally happy and content with my age. It scared me a bit that younger folks began looking to me for "wisdom." But I adapted to that, knowing that sadly, in my next few milestone birthdays, people might forget I still had some. This story is a tribute to all who reach a milestone birthday. Hopefully, I'll remember I wrote it, when I turn 100...

Let's talk antiques. A car can become a collector's items after twenty-five years. A piece of furniture is classified as antique when it's survived a hundred years. Somewhere in the middle of that antique range is another classification—the person who turns fifty years old.

That's me! Last week, I became an antique. Joining an exclusive group of folks who can't quite see that road to retirement or that social security check. Or who just can't see, period. Folks who, these days, are still raising kids, at an age when their parents were welcoming the second or third grandchild (although I think we can wait for that!).

As I awoke on that sunny birthday morn, with the usual aching knees and twitching back, I rolled to the floor and began my little exercise routine. I usually do thirty push ups and thirty sit ups, but thought I'd try to squeeze out fifty push ups that morning. You know, one for each year, just to celebrate. I got to forty and felt I'd celebrated enough. It was a victory for the birthday boy.

Thankfully, shy guy that I am, my fiftieth birthday was fairly uneventful, given the black balloon debacles I've seen others go through.

Oh, there were hundreds of copies of a picture of me at the age of three plastered all over my office at work. And in the hallways. The kitchen. The men's room. Maybe even the ladies room, but I didn't check there. The last guy who turned fifty in our office was popping balloons two at a time to get rid of them all without making a lot of noise. They had covered his office floor. It took him hours. So, I felt lucky with just a smattering of pictures to take down. Boy, I sure was a cute little guy at the age of three . . . with that sport coat, shorts, black socks, and black & white shoes. The Fifties were so hip . . .

My daughter made me a birthday card for the "Big Five O." Envision a mountain peak, if you will, with the number 50 at the top. Coming up the mountain toward the peak, she drew my son and herself. Coming down the mountain on the other side, she drew my wife and myself—Mom first because she has that six months on me that I can tease her about. (Sorry, dear.) It's pure perspective. Kids have it all.

My son presented me with a pair of the most comfortable sandals ever—same kind as the pair he has. The ones I've been borrowing quite often lately. Is that role reversal or what?

My wife's gift was a trip to the theater in Boston to see Mamma Mia, a play built around the hit songs of ABBA, a pop group from the Seventies. A great show. Believe me, there were a lot of "past-the-fiftieth birthday" antiques in that audience.

But I've concluded that the fiftieth birthday is nothing really. Anyone approaching his or her sixtieth will probably agree with me. And it's nothing at all when you've got my childish approach to life—which I hope to maintain as I reach sixty, seventy, maybe eighty pleasant years. When I'm sitting in my wheelchair on the front porch of the Old Folks Home, sucking mashed peas through a straw. And popping all those balloons . . . I wonder what color the balloon makers designate for the eightieth birthday? Hopefully something I'll be able to see.

Two Cents, 7-20-06

The Trial Run

This is another of those nostalgic moments that hit you broadside when you realize the kids will soon be leaving the nest. It doesn't really take all that long to forget that your son backed his car into yours three times in the driveway, over the course of a year. Or took out the corner of the garage and sent a geyser of water spurting into the air when the water pipes snapped. All those downright angry moments become "nostalgic memories" when you realize your child has stepped out that door for good and headed off into the big bad world to take his or her place. Last year, my wife and I had a test run of those things to come. Here's our progress report.

It wasn't any big deal the first night. After all, on occasion, both of the kids have been away overnight at the same time. But, this time, come "Day Three Without Offspring," we started to feel the difference. What struck us most was the quiet. No sound of clacking keystrokes, as our daughter continued her never-ending IM sessions. No booming Surround Sound from the television, as our son and his girlfriend settled in for a night of movies.

We heard no refrigerator door opening, no juice pouring, no ice cubes being cracked from their trays. Never heard the usual night sounds of cars zipping up the driveway, sandals clomping on the front steps, or cell phone chatter from behind closed bedroom doors.

It was eerie, all that silence. And it just didn't feel right.

Five days earlier, we had driven our daughter down to Boston, where she was to attend a 10-day National Youth Leadership Conference on Medicine. A proud moment for us—and also one of those deals where parents spend two grand now so their kids can decide if the medical field is really the career path for them. Good insurance, I suppose, against wasting $150,000 on a pre-med college education when your child suddenly discovers, during a blood drive in her senior year, that she can't stand the sight of blood. This particular send-off was a bittersweet moment for us, but we were happy that Danielle was excited about being at this conference and away for 10 days. Satisfied that she was in good hands, we headed back home.

Three days later, we arose at the crack of dawn, less than bright-eyed and bushy-tailed. That morning, we were headed for the airport to drop off our son—hopefully early enough—to catch a flight to San Diego. With hundreds of other college-level ROTC candidates, he would be spending a month in sunny California, courtesy of the U.S. Navy and Marine Corps. He'd be gone for four weeks, with a tremendous opportunity to investigate whether he wants to stay with the Marine Corps when he graduates or specialize in naval aircraft, ships, or submarines instead. More of a home boy than our daughter, he was a bit hesitant about leaving home that morning. But the excitement of the coming experience drove him on and I bid farewell to this young man who, not long ago was a boy who came up to my waist and now stood eye to eye with me. Well maybe even a bit taller.

My wife and I figured that the exodus of both kids would be an experience for us too. Fewer clothes to wash. Less food to buy. But, on the flip side, there would be no one else with whom to chat about the day's events. And no one else to tease or be teased by. That's important in our family, where we feel that group teasing is a nobler sport than going one-on-one. For a week, there would be no one to challenge me for squatter's rights to the HD TV, or hog the computer, or constantly barge into the bathroom while my wife tries to dry her hair.

So what did we do, the wife and I? Why, we talked to each other more. We ate the food that *we* liked and had dinner late, because we wanted to. We went shopping together for everything from food to electronics to clothes. Okay, I wasn't crazy about the clothes shopping, but still, we did it together. We went to the movies and ate popcorn dripping with that gross imitation butter. Lunch at Panera Bread was in the cards—a first time experience for me. It was like eating in a San Francisco café, for sure, dude. We worked in the garden together and even spent a day at the beach and a night with friends at a quaint dinner party.

I didn't have to dart from the bathroom to the bedroom after a shower, because I forgot a change of underwear. I just took the stroll nonchalantly, and enjoyed the breeze. I wasn't awakened each morning by the sound of my daughter's alarm clock—a wonderful rap "melody" that would annoy even Helen Keller.

*"How can they even **think** about leaving the nest now, Ernie? They're just eggs!" (Photo by Joe Paradis).*

Admittedly, it was a nice five-day respite. Just the two of us. You could write a song about it, if someone hadn't already done so. That little trial run of life after-the-kids-have-gone and before-the-grandchildren-arrive admittedly seems to have some advantages—although I'd like to give the grandchildren scenario about ten more years, thank you. But given our druthers, we're still for having the kids around as long as we can. We might reconsider, of course, if one of them ends up back home at the age of 40, living in the basement after a divorce or bout of unemployment, or something. But we'll take our chances at this point.

So let's all make a pact, shall we, to enjoy those little rascals in our homes for as long as we can. Because once the kids go away to Europe or Iraq or California or Mars or even Derry, their trips back home become progressively shorter and the time between visits progressively longer. Enjoy the minor quarrels over the television set. Relish their time on the cell phone with friends, as they feel comfortable enough to have those conversations while sitting next to you on the couch. Because, before you know it, they're off to find their own way in the world—and no longer in yours.

No Fred Astaire and Ginger Rogers among us, but even I could learn the few steps that kept me from simply dancing in my usual circle pattern. That makes my wife less dizzy. (Photo by Joe Paradis).

Two Cents, 9-14-06

Steppin' Out

Dancing is an art form. And I'd never been too keen on that particular art form. Mostly because I've never known how to dance. Kids in the sixties learned to dance by bouncing up and down. Lots of knee movement. An occasional flailing of the arms. We slow-danced by twirling in a circle. It was dizzying. Twenty years ago, my wife expressed interest in learning how to really dance; I expressed no interest. I was proud of my two left feet. So we never learned—until last year. And it was a blast. I guess I'm getting soft as I age.

"I think we should do it," my wife said, putting the flyer aside.

"Why?" I replied, not highly enthused.

"Because we need to know how to dance," she said. "I'm tired of just going in circles, like we always do, when we try to dance." 'Try' is the operative word here. And she was right. So I agreed. We made arrangements to join CC Mitchell's ballroom dancing class, an adventure that I was sure would live on in the annals of local history.

We'd been contemplating dancing lessons for years. And that's why contemplation is such a great concept—it requires absolutely no action. So we never did commit to it. While I always felt that I'd like to learn how to dance before my kids' weddings (hopefully not for another 10 or 20 years), I just couldn't picture myself with a bunch of middle-aged children of the sixties, trying to learn dance steps from some ancient Arthur Murray dance instructor, sporting a few strands of slicked back hair and smelling of Bay Rum aftershave. We'd, no doubt, gather every Wednesday in some seedy dance hall in downtown Manchester, where our instructor would arrive punctually, decked out in his rather threadbare tuxedo. It seemed like a depressing scenario. Something out of that movie "The Shining."

My dad once tried to teach my sister and me to dance. He himself was an excellent dancer, having grown up in the Big Band Era of the 1940s, when kids just naturally learned how to dance real dances. He chose Christmas Day 1965 to teach us. My sister had just received

Simon & Garfunkel's latest single from Santa. ***The Sounds of Silence***, on a "45" record, for all you oldsters out there. The song began slowly and he thought it was the perfect beat for a foxtrot (or whatever ... what did we know). So my sister and I took turns standing on his feet, as he whirled us around the floor. It was almost as much fun as the slap contests he used to have with my brother and me, as we'd zoom around the kitchen floor in our stocking feet trying to slap one another. Now you know why I'm like I am ...

Anyhow, the dancing lessons ended that day. We quickly fell in with the "generation that couldn't dance." No doubt, we were too busy with schoolwork, charitable activities, and washing dishes every night, to make time for dance lessons. Those were for girlie boys.

But now the wife and I have acquired this yearning to learn how to dance. We needed dancing shoes according to Mr. CC, our instructor. They had to be able to "glide you across the floor." So my wife purchased a pair of official dancing shoes through the Internet. And those, of course, hurt her feet—and my wallet—so she, naturally, purchased a second pair—this time, "dancing sneakers." They apparently did the trick.

In contrast, I did what I usually do when confronted with such decisions—I looked in my closet. There, laying gently on the shoe rack, covered by a protective layer of fine dust, was my pair of tan loafers. Slick as could be on the bottom, tassels and fringe on the top. "Made in Brazil. Tops made of genuine cow leather," read the small print on the bottom. Real Latin Lover gems, these were. I bet I hadn't worn them in five years. Maybe ten. They were perfect. I would glide across that floor like Fred Astaire, with my cutie, Ginger (Joanne) Rogers on my arm. We'd be steppin' out, no doubt, after a few lessons.

But not so fast ... Over the two lessons we've had so far, I've found that dancing takes precision, timing, and coordination—none of which I possess these days in any abundance. However, it takes even more energy to decipher CC's e-mail updates for putting this little dance lesson deal together. It's the risk you take when your dance instructor is a statistician. But the guy can dance. He's been able to point out to me that I really don't have two left feet ... most of the time.

So we approached our first dance lesson a bit timidly. Admitting you stink at something is always a good ice breaker and, with that approach, we met some wonderful people that first class. A couple of ladies from the Senior Center who were looking to "kick up their heals" after many years. A few couples who already knew how to dance, but were looking for a refresher class. And of course, there's always the engineer who has to write down all the steps on a piece of paper to study at home. I liked his attitude.

And we actually had as much fun, that night, as you can have in the basement of a library when you aren't reading. Tripping over our own feet and everyone else's. Bumping into walls and tables, and the very foundation that holds up the building. Stepping on toes. And just generally dragging each other across the floor, much more like Bert and Ernie than Fred and Ginger. No one cared how we looked. Those who could dance helped those of us who had no idea. CC was great. We all laughed at ourselves and each other.

It was a terrific experience.

We quickly learned five dances that we just as quickly forgot by next week's lesson. So we started more slowly the second time. More people showed up too. And darned if I don't at least know a few steps now. It's just a good thing that we'll have 10 to 20 years to teach our kids to dance before their weddings . . . hopefully.

As their career progressed, their looks degraded, according to most parents of the baby boomer generation. But their music will last forever. My kids know almost every Beatles song. (Photo by Joe Paradis).

Two Cents, 12-08-04

The Greatest Band Ever

People will forever debate their favorite "Top Ten" lists—the 100 Best Places to Live, the Top Ten Restaurants, the 50 Most Influential People in the World. In Time magazine's list of that particular category, half are Democrat politicians; the rest are Hollywood actors. Go figure. But in the end, from any list, you still have to choose just one of those that you actually consider to be "the best." In the category of musical bands, I've done that right here. From my selection, you'll know that I'm a Baby Boomer—every generation thinks its music was/is "the best." But 100 years from now, my band's music will still be known. Will yours?

Not long ago, while filling my tank at the gas station, I happened to be humming along to a song that was blasting across the outside speaker. It was some ditty by Blink 182, catchy but nothing special to me. Could have been any one of their two or three hits. "They all sound the same," as my grandfather used to say of my teenage music.

But, as I was closing the gas cap, a teenage kid popped his head around from the other side of the pump and exclaimed, "Aren't they the greatest band ever?" He seemed to be looking for a response.

So I gave him one. "No," I proclaimed, trying to appear a bit sad. I didn't want to hurt his feelings, but I couldn't let him go through life living a lie. "The . . . . are the greatest band ever," I screamed over the din of a passing truck.

"Who?" he screamed back. I repeated my response.

"Oh . . . " he said. "My mom listens to them."

"Your mom's a smart woman," I responded.

I gave him a faux tip of the hat and a knowing smile, and took off. I suspect that I also gave him something to ponder, at least until he pops in his next Blink 182 CD.

On a musical level, I feel sad for our current generation of kids. They just don't have a very good crop of musicians from whom to select "the greatest band ever." Who in their right mind, for example, would choose a hip hop or rap "artist" (there's an oxymoron) as one of "the greatest"? With rare exception, most of those "artists" prefer shock tactics to attract kids, spewing out verbal garbage and a vision of the tough inner city life that might appear cool in a video, but depicts a life few would really want to live.

I doubt that the greatest band would come from any of today's cute little things that pop around on television videos, showing just about "everything they have," except perhaps—for most of them—musical talent. After all, music is auditory, not visual. And while groups like Blink 182, Matchbox 20, Maroon 5, 3 Doors Down (what's with the numbers, by the way?) all have some catchy tunes, I doubt they'll stand the test of time as "the greatest." They would probably fall into the category of earlier groups like The Classics Four, Talking Heads, The Cranberries, Cheap Trick, or The Troggs. Good memories, but not really memorable.

No, the "greatest band ever" needs to be drawn from the ranks of those who paraded their songs across a little device called "radio," something today's CD kids don't know much about. It was in the days of AM radio, when a song was limited to three minutes of airplay, that a band either caught on or it didn't. And the 45 rpm record ruled the day—one song on either side, with the 'A' side being the song most often played. Kids couldn't afford albums, so a band had to have a few hits off an album before a kid actually felt it worthwhile to spend that kind of money. In the early '70s, FM radio gradually allowed for longer songs and songs dealing with issues more serious than just puppy love. The "greatest band ever" has to come from these groups that struggled to compete for that airtime. Today, any "artist" can make a music video. They are far from "the greatest."

The "greatest band ever" also needs to have a variety of talents. Its members can write songs, sing songs, arrange music, and play music. Their music is captivating, the words generally coherent. The ultimate lead singer can usually sing and can often also play guitar, or piano, sometimes drums or saxophone. The ultimate lead guitarist can make a guitar come to life. A quality sax or trumpet player can make the music touch your soul.

Now, there are certainly contenders for the "greatest band ever" from generations earlier than the baby boomers. A number of Big Bands could qualify, as could some of the singers that accompanied them. I would put Louie Armstrong right in there. Frank Sinatra, of course. And Bing Crosby. Maybe Glen Miller, the Andrews Sisters. Much of that earlier music was popular as dance music, and it did the trick. Kids really knew how to dance in those days. Except for songs like the Macarena or the Electric Slide, the Cha Cha Slide or that little step that accompanies Cotton Eyed Joe, teenage dancing since the '60s has consisted primarily of bouncing around.

But the music that really shook a generation—and has now survived a succession of generations—is rock 'n roll. And from that genre comes the "greatest band ever." There are lots of viable contenders for the title. The Rolling Stones. The Eagles. Aerosmith. The Who. Chicago. Pink Floyd. Led Zeppelin. The Supremes. Viable solo performers would include Billy Joel, Elton John, Johnny Cash, Stevie Wonder, Ray Charles, Elvis. There are easily a dozen more. All have had numerous hits that have indeed stood the test of time.

But none of those bands or individuals was as diverse or curious about stretching the boundaries of music, as was the "greatest band ever." None of them matured as quickly from the simple music of three guitars and drums to compositions that included piano, sitar, ukulele, horn and string sections, and even symphonies. They mastered new instruments as they grew. They produced sounds by swishing water in a bucket, by looping short strands of recording tape to repeat a sound over and over. They incorporated the sounds of airplanes, church bells, whistles, and birds into their songs. They played soft ballads and loud rock; wrote silly ditties and made some heavy political statements. They recorded a ton of memorable hits and some junk too. And they eventually imploded, when they began competing with one another, rather than making music together. None was ever as talented on his own, as they were together.

John, Paul, George, and Ringo. The Beatles were "the greatest band ever." Bar none. Listen up, all you kids filling your gas tanks. I'll still be humming their tunes when I'm 64.

I wonder if our Founding Fathers ever encountered "writer's block" when hammering out the Constitution? (Photo by Joe Paradis).

Two Cents, 8-12-04

What to Write About?

People often ask me "How do you come up with this stuff?" I assume they mean the ideas for my stories, although maybe I should ask for clarification from the next person who queries me. But assuming they are referring to my writing, I'll tell you it isn't always easy to come up with something new—especially when you need a fresh idea every week. I find my story ideas in the people and events I observe around me. Then I take a few notes, do a little research for facts, and apply my own dim wit to this mix, before rehashing it several times and finally spitting out something close to what I think will do the trick. In the end, I always hope the story at least makes you chuckle. But once in a while I hit that wall called "writer's block" and just can't think of a thing to write about. And here's what happens...

I am, by nature, a multi-tasker. I like the variety of undertaking several tasks simultaneously and usually completing most of them.

But I haven't the luxury of multitasking tonight. Tonight, I'm under deadline to write this column. Gotta concentrate. Gotta write. I sit down at the kitchen table to begin. But where?

Click. My wife turns on the television. "7 o'clock. Red Sox game's on," she offers.

"Gotta write," I said, glancing for just a second at the TV in the next room. Wakefield's pitching. He's having a tough first inning; Contreras has a perfect inning. 2-0, White Sox. But can't watch... I've gotta write.

Click. "The Olympic Opening Ceremonies are on," my wife says. My daughter drifts in to watch. I glance up once again—just for a moment. A young boy in a huge paper boat floats across the screen, a contrived smile on his face. The paper boat reminds me of the one floating in the gutter in the Steven King movie "It." The boy is waving to 100,000 people from the middle of a huge pool in the center of the

Olympic Stadium. He's waving to millions more watching on TV. But, I can't watch. Gotta write.

Click. "Just checking the Patriots-Eagles pre-season game," Joanne calls out. I also thought I heard a giggle from the TV room. That's pressure.

"Gotta write!" I yell out. But, darn, Brady looks good. A few passes and the Pats are on the 12-yard line. The Eagles just committed their sixth penalty. Thank you, guys. Thank you.

Click. Some guy in his underwear is balancing on a cube suspended over the Olympic Stadium. Those Greeks . . .

Click. Manny hits his 29th home run, tying the game 4-4. I love that goofy guy. But gotta concentrate. Gotta write.

Click. Yes! Dillon just scores a touchdown, with four minutes left in the first quarter. 7-0 Pats. It's starting to pour in Foxboro. Good God, help me write!

Click. Some guy just rips the dress off a young woman, who bounds out into the water in the middle of the Olympic Stadium. What are these people doing? Someone says it's "art." Where is that boy in the paper boat?

Click. New quarterback Rohan Davey replaces Brady. Oh! What was that? Yesssss, Vinateri kicks a field goal! 10-0 Pats.

Click. Looks like Cupid or Tinkerbell floating over the Stadium now. Somersaulting in the air above what looks like an army of headless green mannequins. Good Lord. This is the Olympics?

Click. Arghhh. Wakefield just gives up two runs. Get the bum out of there. Francona must have heard me; here he comes to yank Wake.

Click. Another woman strolls into that wading pool in the Olympic Stadium. She's apparently pregnant and suddenly her belly starts to glow. The announcer spouts something about symbolism. Can I possibly write about a glowing stomach at the Olympics?

Click. Ooooops . . . what's this? 10-3 Pats. There goes the shut out. Can't let up on those Eagles. Nice tackle, Izzo!

Click. Yeeeaaahh, Manny! A double off the wall. And another run! You go, Ortiz! 6-5 White Sox. A run at a time, guys. Be patient. What the heck can I write about?

Click. "The athletes will enter the Stadium in alphabetic order by country, according to the Greek alphabet," blares the official announcer.

"All announcements will be made in Greek first, then French, then English." Whaaaaat? French before English? And what about Spanish, the second most popular language in the Western Hemisphere—behind English? It's those French again. I swear... still trying to rule the world.

Click. Pat's still 10-3 at halftime.

Click. White Sox. 8, Red Sox 5. What happened? Oh, no, not Mendoza pitching...

Click. " ... and now, the athletes from United Arab Republic, followed by the United States." There we are, backing up our Arab friends again. Nothing but cheers from the crowd. Are they clapping for the UAR or the USA? Let's assume both. For the sake of humanity.

Click. " ... and the Red Sox lose by the score of 8-7."

Click. " ... and the Patriots beat Philadelphia, 24-6!"

Click. " ... and next is the country of Lesotho." Lesotho? Never heard of that country. Their one athlete looks lonely. Wait, wait... there's only one athlete from Liechtenstein too. Maybe they can form their own country together.

The Patriots, the Red Sox, and the Summer Olympics. The good, the bad, and the ugly. And still, I have nothing to write about...

The pendulum seems to have swung against the Yankees temporarily, as it did in 2004. But never overestimate the power of gloating ... it'll bite you sooner or later, when the team you dislike comes roaring back. (Photo by Joe Paradis).

Two Cents, 5-06-04

Shamelessly Gloating

In the spring of 2004, the Boston Red Sox were on the way to their most glorious year ever, culminating in Boston's first World Series win in 86 years. Throughout all those years, the Red Sox and New York Yankees have been arch-rivals. But before that magical year, it had always been next to impossible for either team to sweep the other- especially in the rival's ballpark. So when the Sox did exactly that in May of 2004—marching into Yankee Stadium and "taming the tiger"—I just had to write about it. But the rivalry is never one-sided. In 2006, the Yankees returned the favor, all but pushing the Sox out of post-season contention, with a sweep at Fenway Park. And in 2007, the Sox reversed that once again, burying the Yankees deep early in the season, but watching them roar back later. I love this stuff—and I gloat when I can. But I'm leery. I know pendulums swing both ways... especially in baseball.

Allow me, if you will, a moment of gloating. Gloat, gloat, gloat, gloat, gloat. How's about just one more time—G...L...O...A...T!

Thank you for your indulgence. I'm just giddy from it all. 4 ½ games up on the Evil Empire. Winners of 5 out of 6. A 3-game sweep in the Big Apple. Can it get any better than that for baseball's greatest rivalry? Especially when it's the Red Sox over the Yankees in such commanding fashion? Gloat, gloat, gloat, gloat, gloat!

Now, I'll admit it's still early in the season. But if the Yankees had swept the Sox last weekend, you'd have heard nothing but how powerful their line up is, how sharp their pitching, how worthwhile the $183 million payroll. Personally, I preferred hearing these little gems. "Jeter has gone 0 for 25 in his last six games." "The Yanks are batting .132 so far this year." Or my favorite from Mr. Jeter himself "We haven't played well. [The booing from New York fans] shows they really care." That's precious!

There were **some** fans having a good time at Yankee Stadium last weekend. Oh, excuse me, those were **Red Sox** fans. I should have known by that familiar cheer "Let's go Red Sox! Let's go Red Sox!" I was particularly gratified by the picture in last week's Union Leader of a guy from New Jersey holding up a sign that proclaimed "SWEEP!" From a Jersey local! Someone who lives 5 miles from Yankee Stadium. I don't think he was the janitor either.

Watch this little tap dance! Tap, tap, tap, tap tap.

Now, of course, these are just my emotions running away with me. Because, in all probability, unless something really drastic happens, these two teams will meet again in the fall, when every game really counts. They still have another 13 games to play against one another this season. And I do recall the words of that old philosopher, Manny Ramirez, uttered just a week ago. "The objective here is to win the World Series, not beat the Yankees. They're the ones who got the rings. We don't got nothing." Such perspective. Such insight. Such . . . command of the double negative. But I think I know what he meant.

In the meantime, follow me kids. Indulge your own whim. Give me a "Good God Almighty!" We just can't get as excited as this when the Sox beat Seattle. Or Cleveland. Or Texas. Oh, we can smirk a little bit at this point, when we recall how a team named for a fish actually beat New York in last year's World Series. But all that pales next to a Red Sox sweep of the Yankees in their own ballpark.

Gloat, gloat, gloat, gloat, gloat.

About the Author

Joseph Robert Paradis was born in Arlington, Massachusetts in 1954, the second of four children. With good grades and an incessant sense of humor, he was able to both please and dismay the St. Joseph nuns who taught him through twelve years of parochial school. He served in the U.S. Air Force, before obtaining a BS degree in Business Management from Suffolk University and an MBA from Boston University. He moved to Londonderry, New Hampshire in 1984 and in 2004, began writing a weekly humor column for his local community newspaper, *The Londonderry Times*. That column, **Joe's Two Cents**, earned him the Humor Columnist of the Year award for both 2005 and 2006, from the New Hampshire Press Association. Its stories are the basis for this book.

Joe's ultimate desire is to spread the news that humor is a tremendous trait and should be present in all aspects of our lives. He is currently developing seminars to this affect, particularly on humor in the workforce, and expects to soon teach creative writing and humor in an educational environment as well.

Joe still lives in Londonderry, New Hampshire with his wife of twenty-three years, Joanne, and their children, Robert and Danielle, who are both ready to spread their own wings soon. To correspond with Joe, schedule a seminar, or order additional copies of this book, visit his Web site at www.joes2cents.com. And smile while you're doing that, will ya?